# JOSEPH HAWLEY

# JOSEPH HAWLEY
## COLONIAL RADICAL

BY
E. FRANCIS BROWN

AMS Press, Inc.
New York
1966

AMS Press, Inc.
New York, N.Y. 10003
1966

Manufactured in the United States of America

TO
MY PARENTS

## PREFACE

Joseph Hawley was one of the most remarkable men produced by western Massachusetts in the eighteenth century. Although born and reared under what were practically frontier conditions and influences, he surpassed most of his contemporaries in breadth of vision and liberalism in matters of politics and religion. In the struggle between the royal power and the Massachusetts radicals he played a leading part. Unafraid of the circumstances, he urged all measures which seemed to make for political liberty, and was not frightened by the possibility of actual fighting with, or separation from, Great Britain. Small wonder that by his contemporaries he was called a "river god." Unfortunately at the height of his career, he was overwhelmed by the family taint of insanity and retired from public life forever. If health had been permitted to him, it seems almost certain that he would have played a leading part after 1776, not only in Massachusetts, but in the country at large.

I first learned of Joseph Hawley when, as a boy in Northampton, I read eagerly the history of that town and the surrounding countryside. Joseph Hawley's real importance, however, I never fully appreciated until it was called to my attention a few years ago by Professor Evarts B. Greene of Columbia University. From that time I hoped to be able to write the biography of Hawley; the present little volume is the realization of that hope. Working with the materials of Hawley's life I have come to feel strongly that any man of importance is in most respects only a reflection of his times. For this reason it may seem that I have often neglected Joseph Hawley for political or social events, that the background envelops the subject of the portrait; yet only in this way, I am certain, can any sort of proper perspective be gained. After all, the Massachusetts stage in the eighteenth century was crowded with many characters—some were prominent actors, others were only scene-shifters. Where Joseph Hawley stands in relation to them is answered perhaps in this, his first biography.

I am still unable to understand why the life of Hawley has not been written before. His contemporaries had a high opinion of him; he is mentioned at length in the lives of Elbridge Gerry, James Otis and James Sullivan, and is given considerable notice by Thomas Hutchinson in the third volume of his *History of Massachusetts Bay*. George Bancroft was enough interested in Hawley to include the family papers in his vast collection of source material on American history. One wonders whether Bancroft contemplated the eventual writing of a biography. In talking with many historians of the present day I have been further mystified by encountering a good deal of interest in Hawley, the frequently expressed hope that a biography would be written, and yet no one who seemed ready to undertake the task.

My study and research in preparation of this biography have taken me into many aspects of Massachusetts history. I have come to realize that there is genuine need for an adequate history of the great Commonwealth, a history which will interpret in proper perspective the interplay of social, economic and political forces. Most of all there is need for a history which will recognize that colonial Boston was not all of Massachusetts, that the western part of the province was an important, self-conscious entity whose representatives were influential in shaping the work of the General Court. Such a history also would give emphasis to the Loyalists and Shays' Rebellion—two phases of eighteenth century Massachusetts history which to my mind are still neglected.

# PREFACE

My researches carried me to the New York Public Library, the Columbia University Library, the Forbes Library at Northampton, the Massachusetts Historical Society at Boston and the Widener Library at Harvard University—at all of them the staffs were most kind with their patient assistance. I am grateful also for the courtesy extended to me by officials of the Hampshire County Court House at Northampton, the City Clerk's office at Northampton, the Suffolk County Court House at Boston, and especially by the staff of the Archives Department in the Massachusetts State House. Miss Clara Hudson of Northampton and Plainfield, Mass.—a descendant of Joseph Hawley's adopted son—graciously permitted me to use some of the family papers and to view the few remaining personal possessions of Joseph Hawley. Many friends whom I would like to name helped my study by their constant encouragement and sympathetic criticism. Mr. Spencer Brodney, a friend and associate, read my manuscript and was of great assistance in smoothing many awkward passages; I alone am responsible for the many which remain. My former colleague, Professor Robert E. Riegel of Dartmouth College, also read the manuscript and made many helpful suggestions. My thanks are due especially to Professor Evarts B. Greene of Columbia University who has advised, encouraged and criticized my work throughout its progress; his inspiration has guided me over many rough and troublesome places.

E. FRANCIS BROWN

New York City,
July, 1931

## CONTENTS

| | | |
|---|---|---|
| Preface | . . . . . . . . . . . . | vii |
| I. | His Heritage . . . . . . . . . | 1 |
| II. | The Formative Years . . . . . . | 8 |
| III. | The Edwards Affair . . . . . . . | 24 |
| IV. | Attorney and Barrister . . . . . . | 42 |
| V. | A "River God" . . . . . . . . . | 69 |
| VI. | At the "Parliament of Massachusetts Bay" | 96 |
| VII. | The Sons of Liberty . . . . . . . | 116 |
| VIII. | A Leader of Massachusetts . . . . | 141 |
| IX. | Reconstruction . . . . . . . . | 173 |
| X. | At the Last . . . . . . . . . | 190 |
| Bibliography | . . . . . . . . . . | 193 |
| Index | . . . . . . . . . . . . | 209 |

## Chapter I

## HIS HERITAGE

The year was 1723 and the month October, in that section of the New World the most glorious season of the year. Already the nearby hills and valleys were ablaze with the brilliant reds and yellows of the autumn foliage while the swamplands and the roadsides were flaming with the crimson of the sumachs. Harvest time was nearly over; men were thinking of threshing, of fall plowing and of the winter that all too soon would imprison them. Such was the setting of the frontier town of Northampton in His Majesty's province of Massachusetts Bay. His Majesty, far away at St. James's or whatever royal residence his fancy had selected at the moment, was the German-speaking George I, homesick for his native Hanover, knowing little and undoubtedly caring less about the extremely distant province in America. His deputy in the province, Lieutenant-Governor William Dummer, was preoccupied in Boston by a chronic dispute with the fractious General Court and on the northern frontiers by the obstinate sputtering of Father Râle's War. Neither king nor governor cared about Northampton, and that town in turn showed but the slightest interest in Father Râle's War and knew George I only as a name on official documents and proclamations.

As the Northampton men went about their work, breathing in the spicy tang that belongs only to the air of a New England fall, they gloried in the delight of a bright, clear sun, still hot at midday but no longer penetrating to the cool damp of shaded spots. The hills and mountains which by shutting Northampton off from the rest of the world gave it a character of its own, were bathed in a blue haze that gave notice of the approaching Indian summer; at their feet wound a deep blue ribbon, the Connecticut river with its great bends and ox-bows.

But the people of Northampton had little time to appreciate the beauties of nature. Their lives were concerned chiefly with the problems of maintaining existence. If anyone thought of nature it was not of her wondrous beauty but her lavish bounty; one might marvel at the great stretches of meadowland on either side of the river, rich land, low-lying, and fertile with ages of alluvial deposit; or rejoice in the seemingly unlimited supply of timber and firewood in the forests which covered the regions to the west of the town; rolling country which ever mounting higher stretched across the trackless miles to Albany. At times some may have wished that nature or fate had not separated Northampton from the other parts of Massachusetts Bay by such long, lonely stretches of forest road; but most went about their business, considering only the nearest issues of life.

The housewives at their tasks on one of those October days were gossiping about an event in Pudding Lane; there was a new baby at the Joseph Hawley's. New babies were not rare in the prolific days of eighteenth-century Northampton, but when this boy was born on October 8, 1723, to one of the leading families of the community, born to position and a worthy tradition, it was something to gossip about. If the housewives could have seen ahead a half century they might well have talked even more, but without the gift of foresight, they were forced back upon a contemplation of the infant's ancestors and parents.

His grandfather Hawley, the first Joseph, had come to Northampton in 1674 when the town was only twenty years old and its crablike plan of streets and lanes had only begun to develop. He was fresh from Harvard then, and anxious to start earning a livelihood, if only by teaching school. So he taught for ten years, preached, too, sometimes, for he was a licensed preacher, until gradually secular affairs got the upper hand and this first Joseph Hawley turned his back upon the professions. Not entirely, however, because without studying law he practised it, and for years conducted every suit to which the town of Northampton was a party. Through these years he grew in importance and influence until Governor Andros considered him prominent enough to appoint him a justice of Hampshire County. When Andros' régime was over and the province had a new charter, Hawley was again appointed a justice of the peace and an associate justice of the Court of General Sessions. He held, besides, a commission as lieutenant in the militia and found time in the press of public duties to carry on a diversified mercantile business that ranged from Indian trading to the selling of the inevitable rum and of Mrs. Rowlandson's account of her captivity among the Indians.[1]

During the years when he was building up a reputation for integrity and public spirit, he played an active rôle in raising the little settlement of 1674 into an important center. To be sure, its actual population was not great, and this first Joseph Hawley would be long in his grave before the town could number a thousand inhabitants. Yet it shared with Springfield, twenty miles down the river, the honor of holding the court of Hampshire County when periodically the justices and lawyers gathered at some Northampton tavern to hear cases and to render justice in the king's name, but with all due consideration for the importance of Massachusetts Bay. People rode in from the surrounding towns for these court sessions. Some ferried

[1] J. R. Trumbull, *History of Northampton*, I, 524-31. Trumbull based his history very largely upon the Judd Manuscript, a vast collection of source material which is now in the Forbes Library at Northampton. The collection consists of reminiscences, extracts from diaries, journals, account books, observations, official records and the like. In many ways Trumbull's history is itself only a compilation of sources as any one who goes over the records of Northampton history will quickly discover.

across the river from Hadley, the little town whose brief history contained the romantic legend of two judges of Charles I; others rode the four or five miles from Hatfield, on the river just above Northampton; and still others came from battlescarred and tomahawked Deerfield, their minds still filled with the horrors of the massacre of 1704.

These court visitors found nothing unusual in the town's appearance for it closely resembled all others with which they were familiar. Set on Meeting-house hill, a gentle slope to the center of the town, was the church which served both religious and secular needs. Except for a tiny schoolhouse it held the distinction of being the only public building, but in 1723 it was old and fast falling into decay. The dwellings on the streets or lanes which straggled out from the meetinghouse were generally of frame construction, clapboarded and unpainted, the elements soon weathering them to a dreary brown. Some betrayed the English inheritance of their builders in the projecting upper story which popular tradition in a later age believed to be devised to ward off Indian attacks. They had no porches and faced broadside and close to the streets, giving to the front entrance, in that day when sidewalks were unknown, the appropriate name of street door. Close to the house and bordering the street was the inevitable barn from which manure and other waste were thrown into the thoroughfare. Yet town and dwelling met the requirements of living in an age that had little time for aesthetic frills.[2]

The first Joseph Hawley died in 1711, after being gored by an ox, but he left a son, also named Joseph, who after receiving two thirds of his father's estate, began in his turn to establish a reputation in the town. A man of ability and culture, although without college training, he soon made his mark. For nineteen years he was one of the town selectmen and frequently the town clerk. Like his father he carried the title of lieutenant and found time to look after wide and diversified business interests. For years

[2] Trumbull, *op. cit.*, II, 1-5.

he was the principal trader in town and cattle-drover between the region about Northampton and the metropolis at the Bay. In his store could be purchased the dry goods of the time, silk handkerchiefs, the powder and lead so essential in early eighteenth century life, pipes for men and women, and most wonderful of all, table knives and forks. He had a large farm to manage, an interest in a sawmill to think of, and as if this were not enough, he carried on boating on the Connecticut river, the great avenue for transporting bulky goods. Certainly in some respects eighteenth century economic life could be complex. With such a diversity of interests, one might think that this second Joseph would have had little time for introspection, but a vein of melancholy in his nature, coupled with a deep religious sense, made him the victim of a terrifying self-analysis.[3]

If the Hawley heritage assured the new baby, the third Joseph, a high position in Northampton life, it was doubly assured by the heritage from his mother's people. His maternal grandfather was the Reverend Solomon Stoddard, for nearly sixty years the pastor of the Northampton church and the leader of the churches of western Massachusetts; Pope Stoddard, his opponents called him. This tall, spare, impressive figure was stern and sedate, yet courteous and affable. Moreover he was a man of great learning and piety and one of the few in the town whose wide contacts gave him a broad outlook. Among his close friends was Samuel Sewall from whom he received periodic gifts of "chokolat," "reasons" and almonds, and at the death of one of Sewall's successive wives, Stoddard's letter of condolence caused the forlorn widower to be soaked in tears.[4] At Stoddard's home, known even today as "The Manse," was a large library and his cherished belongings included ten table knives and nine forks.[5] Here he kept open house

[3] *Ibid.*, II, 78-82.
[4] *Diary of Samuel Sewall*, (Mass. Hist. Soc. Coll., Series. 5, V-VIII), II, 153.
[5] Trumbull, *op. cit.*, II, 52-66.

to visitors and friends from all over the province, and probably Samuel Sewall was not the only guest who was so well entertained that he thought Northampton "a very Paradise."

Solomon Stoddard's eleventh child, Rebekah, was the boy Joseph's mother. Well educated for her day, possessed of tremendous energy, she was a woman of decision and will. Possibly her late marriage to the second Joseph Hawley is an evidence of her independent mind. She was thirty-six when she became Rebekah Hawley. In later life she became famous in the valley as a maker of butter and especially cheese. As the daughter of Solomon Stoddard, her social position was assured and with a naturally aristocratic spirit was combined a trait of eccentricity that as the years passed furnished the village gossips with items of never failing interest.[6]

Of all the family, however, the most interesting and in some respects the most prominent was Rebekah's brother, John Stoddard. While he might be called "a cussed lazy devil" by his enemies, he came, largely through land speculation, to be one of the wealthiest men in town and for a long time he owned the only gold watch of which the town could boast. In 1723 much of his public life was still ahead of him; behind were many years of Indian fighting. If pressed, he could tell of that terrible night of the Indian attack on Deerfield in 1704 when he leaped from the second story of Parson Williams' house to race barefoot across the snow for help from Hatfield. Later he had gone among the Papists at Quebec to ransom English captives, and now in 1723 was a colonel in the militia.[7] The years were to bring him prominence and honors in the military, judicial and legislative fields, and the historian of the province was to write of him: "There have been but few men who have been more generally esteemed."[8]

[6] Trumbull, *op. cit.*, II, 82-83.
[7] *Ibid.*, II, 165-78.
[8] Thomas Hutchinson, *History of Massachusetts Bay*, II, 386.

When the townspeople at their simple meals on that October day talked of the new Hawley baby and of his family, they talked of one of themselves. The Stoddards might have slight pretensions to aristocracy, but not the Hawleys, and even the Stoddards could not put on aristocratic airs in the rough atmosphere of frontier Northampton. There was no silver spoon in this infant's mouth in spite of his parents' comfortable social and economic position. Born in the midst of frontier democracy, he was always to be a part of it.

Before long there was a second son in the Hawley household, Elisha, born on July 18, 1726. Throughout the years, Joseph was devoted to this younger brother and his love never slackened, however sorely it might be tried by Elisha's waywardness. Time was to show that the younger brother lacked stability and solidity, and while he must have caused his family many heartburnings, he was favored throughout his brief life with that consideration which is lavished only on a younger son.

As the Hawley babies in the following years learned to observe life and objects about them, they found that family life centered in their mother's kitchen, a fairly pleasant place which closely resembled all the other kitchens of the village. There was the great fireplace with its innumerable hooks and pots and kettles. Above it the mantle held pewter candlesticks, the tinder box and at times the Bible. As they learned to toddle about the house, through the wainscoted rooms with their uncarpeted but sanded floors and up the narrow winding stairway opposite the front door, they must have explored the mysteries of the spinning wheel and their mother's loom. Perhaps in the early process of learning they marveled at the patterns the diamond-shaped window panes cast on the floor or tried to work the latch string in the great nail-studded, oaken front door.[9] Soon, however, life passed beyond their father's house and Joseph, with Elisha tagging along, began the first steps towards capitalizing the gifts of his heritage.

[9] Trumbull, *op. cit.*, II, 2-9.

CHAPTER II

## THE FORMATIVE YEARS

Life in Northampton in the early eighteenth century must have been rather drab and bleak, although for boys there were constant diversions and excitements. Ever in their minds were stories of Indian fighting and fears of new wars to come. There were stories of the fierce animals in the woods to the west and on the nearby mountains, and frequently on cold, still winter nights, the howling of wolves could be heard in the little town. But much of life was more homely than all that. There was the time-honored sport, with barefoot boys, of throwing stones through the church, or better still the schoolhouse windows, much to the dismay of the town fathers.[1] It was good fun, also, to let down the bars of a neighbor's fence so that his cows or horses would wander out. In the spring there was fishing for salmon and shad in the river where the ferry crossed to Hockanum, fishing with nets that brought in thousands of salmon and shad in a single day. Eels were very plentiful in the Mill river which ran through the town and every young boy occasionally went out at night with the older men, holding a birchbark torch while they speared the eels which were attracted by the light.[2]

On Sunday church was inescapable, two long and wearisome sessions at which Grandfather Stoddard preached without notes, and after 1726, Joseph's much older cousin, Jonathan Edwards, alternately terrified and enthralled the congregation. But if contemporary records can be relied upon, the children did their best to lighten the hours of

[1] Trumbull, *op. cit.*, II, 165-78.
[2] S. Judd, *History of Hadley*, pp. 313-17.

divine worship. Six tithingmen were needed to keep order in 1738 and more could have been used.³ One church meeting probably long remained in Joseph's memory. It was March 13, 1737, the old church was crowded, and Jonathan Edwards was getting well under way his sermon on the text, "Behold ye despisers and wonder and perish." Suddenly a clap like thunder filled the meeting house and amid shrieking and wailing the front gallery with its seventy or more occupants fell to the floor. But Providence, as Edwards wrote later, disposed of every timber so that none in the gallery nor in the seats below was seriously injured.⁴

In the previous Autumn, the construction of a new meetinghouse, much larger and more elegant than the old, had begun. Its raising must have been watched by Joseph and Elisha and their playmates. A joyous raising it was; the timbers were put into place with the assistance of sixty-nine gallons of rum, thirty-six pounds of sugar, together with several barrels of cider and beer. Small wonder that Deacon Ebenezer Hunt wrote in his diary: "We finished the raising of the house, and we have abundant cause to take notice with thankfulness of the kindness of God to us in protecting and preserving the lives and limbs of all those that were active in the building of the house."⁵ Such festive occasions interested small boys little less than the exciting moments of the frequent fires in the town. Without organized fire protection and at a time of almost universal wooden construction a fire was nearly certain to be very spectacular and enjoyable if the more serious elements involved were forgotten.

When Joseph was eleven years old the town experienced a religious revival of a soul-searching nature. It was the beginning of the Great Awakening. The boy's father was so profoundly affected that in despair he did away with him-

³ Trumbull, *op. cit.*, II, 77.
⁴ *Ibid.*, II, 75-76. Also noted in the diary of Deacon Ebenezer Hunt in the Judd Manuscript I, 27, Forbes Library, Northampton, Mass.
⁵ *Ibid.*, II, 70.

self. Jonathan Edwards tells of this episode in his vivid account of the revival:

> In the latter part of May, it began to be very sensible that the spirit of God was gradually drawing from us, and after this time Satan seemed to be more let loose, and raged in a dreadful manner. The first instance, wherein it appeared, was a person's putting an end to his own life, by cutting his throat. He was a gentleman of more than common understanding, of strict morals, religious in his behavior, and an useful, honorable person in the town; but was of a family that are exceeding prone to the disease of melancholy, and his mother was killed with it. He had from the beginning of this extraordinary time, been exceedingly concerned about the state of his soul, and there were some things in his experience, that appeared very hopefully, but he durst entertain no hope concerning his own estate. Towards the latter part of his time, he grew much discouraged and melancholy grew amain upon him, till he was wholly overpowered by it, and was in great measure, past a capacity of receiving advice, or being reasoned with to any purpose. The devil took the advantage and drove him into despairing thoughts. He was kept awake nights, meditating terror, so that he had scarce any sleep at all, for a long time together. And it was observed at last, that he was scarcely well capable of managing his ordinary business and was judged delirious by the coroner's inquest.[6]

Through the years of boyhood Joseph was attending the town schools and digesting the frugal fare they offered. The teachers, generally Harvard graduates, fresh from college and on their way to the ministry, were poorly paid. The schoolmaster in 1726 received only £48. Two years later the schoolmaster was Dr. Samuel Mather who was also the town surgeon.[7] Under these masters a boy learned to read, write, and cast accounts, while in the higher or grammar schools he learned the rudiments of English and

---

[6] J. Edwards, *Narrative of Surprizing Conversions*, p. 74. Deacon Ebenezer Hunt wrote in his diary: "June 1, 1735—Lt. Joseph Hawley cut his throat & took away his own life. It was Lord's day morning. He lived about half an hour after it, but did not speak. An awful Providence." Judd Manuscript, I, 24.

[7] Trumbull, *op. cit.*, II, 85.

## FORMATIVE YEARS

Latin grammar. The books in the Hawley home were not particularly interesting. Even an eighteenth century boy could find little fascination in Hunt's *Explanation on Daniel*, Dr. Mather's *Entrance into the Kingdom of Heaven*, or Willard's *Truly Blessed Man*. But when Joseph had learned sufficient Latin, he could turn to his father's old volumes of Vergil's works and Cicero's *Orations*. There was a volume on military discipline that may have had some interest and his grandfather's old *Rules of Pleading* which perhaps had a sentimental fascination.[8] After leaving the grammar school the boy may have studied for some time under Jonathan Edwards. It was customary for boys preparing for college to work at least for a while with the minister; his kinship with Edwards and his intention to enter Yale College, Edwards' alma mater, make it even more likely. At any rate in 1739 when not quite sixteen years old, Joseph was ready to start the two-day trip which would bring him to the orthodox institution of learning at New Haven.

The influence of Jonathan Edwards had doubtless decided the boy's matriculation at Yale, although Hawley's attention would naturally have been drawn to the institution where Elisha Williams, a native of Hatfield, was just retiring from a service of thirteen years as its president. The presence at Yale of several Northampton youths may well have influenced him further. In the class of 1740 were two Northampton boys, Ezra Clap and Thomas Strong, and in the Yale classes of the early 1740's were other boys from Northampton and the nearby towns. In the eighteenth century New Haven was much more accessible from western Massachusetts than Boston. A journey to the Massachusetts capital meant an arduous trip on horseback through long stretches of wilderness, but New Haven could be reached by a trip down the Connecticut river and through well-settled country. Possibly, too, as

[8] Books listed in the inventory of Lt. Joseph Hawley's estate, 1735. Hampshire County Probate Records.

many of the settlers of the region had come from the Connecticut towns, there was still more communication with them than with the towns and villages to the eastward. Yale as a safely orthodox institution was very likely to be preferred to Harvard with its religious uncertainties. Certain it was that of the fifty-three Massachusetts boys who were graduated from Yale during the years between the opening of the college and 1745, forty-two came from Hampshire County.[9]

New Haven in 1739 was only a small town, a cluster of houses about a village green, and Joseph Hawley could not have been greatly impressed. The college by this time was firmly established and, in contrast with its condition twenty years earlier, was prosperous. The one building, itself called the college, stood at the corner of what are today College and Chapel Streets, and was a large barrack-like structure. Its steep roof was broken at intervals by dormers and in the center was a belfry. In Hawley's time the college was probably unpainted, although by 1750 it had been painted blue. This building contained the chapel which also served as a dining hall, the library with its twenty-six hundred volumes, and suites to accomodate sixty-six students. The kitchen was in a low ell attached to the main structure.[10]

College bills were not excessive. Tuition was fixed in 1737 at sixty shillings a year and a like sum covered the fees of graduation. While board and room varied constantly, in 1730 it was only six shillings a week.[11] However, if the menu drawn up in 1741 can be accepted, the college commons did not offer sybarite fare. Breakfast was to consist of one loaf of bread for four persons; dinner, also for four, was a little less Spartan: one loaf of bread, two and a half pounds of beef, veal or mutton, or perhaps in

[9] F. B. Dexter, *Biographical Sketches of Graduates of Yale College*, I, 773.
[10] Dexter, *op. cit.*, I, 198.
[11] *Ibid.*, I, 570, 550, 401.

## FORMATIVE YEARS

the summer time one and three quarters pounds of salt pork about twice a week, one quart of milk, and two pennyworth of sauce. Supper, nearly as light as breakfast, found a loaf of bread and two quarts of milk on the table. But if milk could not be had conveniently an apple pie made according to the following recipe might be substituted: one and three quarters pounds of dough, a quarter pound of hog's fat, two ounces of sugar, and one peck of apples.[12] Such meals must have caused many a student to break college regulations and spend his pocket money at the bakeshop or tavern.

Entrance to Yale depended on a knowledge of the classics, but apparently all that an applicant needed to know was Vergil, part of Cicero's *Orations*, and the four Evangelists in Greek. Freshmen studied Greek and Hebrew the first four days of the week; rhetoric, oratory, divinity, "both tongues," the arts and some authors, the latter part. Upperclassmen studied rhetoric, logic, theology, metaphysics, elementary mathematics and the ancient languages. Every student declaimed once in six weeks.[13] The training was thus solidly classical although the college library made possible some self-education in modern literature. Largely through the gift from the philosopher Berkeley, of nearly one thousand volumes in 1733, the Yale library had a better collection of modern works than Harvard. This donation included the best of English literature—Shakespeare, Francis Bacon, Pope, Gay, and Swift for example.[14] The library also contained Locke, Hooker, Clarendon's History, bound sets of the *Spectator* and *Tatler*, as well as Montaigne, Bayle, Machiavelli and Cervantes.[15] Just how great was student use of the library is difficult to determine. In 1743 the college

---

[12] *Ibid.*, I, 663.

[13] *Ibid.*, I, 347.

[14] T. G. Wright, *Literary Culture in Early New England 1620-1730*, pp. 184-87.

[15] Dexter, *op. cit.*, I, 723-24.

published a catalogue of the library and recommended that the students follow a regular course of studies by using this catalogue. Possibly the Rector was trying to stimulate greater use of the library.

The daily routine of the students began with morning prayer at six, between March 10 and September 10, and at sunrise during the rest of the year. This regimen possibly served to remind them that "every student shall consider the main end of his study to wit to know God in Jesus Christ and answerably to lead a Godly sober life."[16] Freedom away from the college was limited to short periods after meals. For the rest the student was expected to "studiously observe his time observing both the Laws Common for the students to meet in the hall and those that are appointed to his own lectures which he shall diligently attend and be inoffensive in his attendance thereunto in word and gesture."[17] While the rules forbade visits to taverns and other eating places, it seems rather doubtful if these were any more carefully observed than the stringent regulations against drinking. College rules down through the centuries apparently have been made to be broken and those of eighteenth century Yale were probably no exception.

Student life has always had a raucous, riotous side, and the boys at Yale—the average was graduated at twenty-one—could scarcely be expected to be more exemplary than the rest of their species. A letter of Hawley's fellow-townsman, Ezra Clap, throws a beam of light across the Yale of 1738:

Last night some of the freshman got six quarts of Rhum and about two payls fool of Sydar and about eight pounds sugar and mad it into Samson, and evited every Scholar in Colege into Churtis is Room, and we mad such prodigious Rought that we raised the tutor, and he ordered us all to our one rooms and some went and some taried and they gathered again and went up old father Monsher dore and

[16] *Ibid.*, I, 347.
[17] *Ibid.*, I, 347.

## FORMATIVE YEARS 15

drummed against the dore and yeled and screamed so that a bodey would have thought that they were killing [dogs] there, and all this day they have been a counseling to geather and they sent for Woodward and Dyar and Worthenton, Briant and Styles.[18]

Such parties were probably not uncommon and Hawley may well at times have been among those who tarried and gathered again.

One episode of Hawley's college life must have been long remembered. In October, 1740, George Whitefield the revivalist spent three days in New Haven and preached several times in the meetinghouse on the green. Great crowds rode in from the countryside to hear him and in the front gallery of the church were the students of the college listening to what seemed to be truly inspired preaching.[19] Of the college Whitefield wrote in his journal, "It is about one-third part as big as that of Cambridge [Harvard]. It has one Rector, three Tutors, and about a hundred students. I hear of no remarkable concern among them regarding religion."[20] The winter following Whitefield's visit was intensely cold and towards its end, when tempers had worn thin, the college was swept by a religious revival which today is recognized as a minor episode in the Great Awakening. It threw Yale into a turmoil which lasted for several years; theological and religious discussion diverted all thoughts from studies, and to the elders it seemed as if the new attitude towards religion was undermining all respect for authority. In an attempt to curb the new enthusiasm the trustees voted "that if any Student of this College shall directly or indirectly say, that the Rector, either of the Trustees or Tutors, are hypocrites, carnal or unregenerate men, he shall for the first offense make a public confession in the Hall, and for the second offence be expelled."[21] Expulsions did follow only to intensify the

[18] F. B. Dexter, *Documentary History of Yale University*, p. 351.
[19] J. N. Reynolds, *Two Centuries of Christian Activity at Yale*, p. 19.
[20] W. Wale, edit., *George Whitefield's Journals*, p. 482.
[21] Dexter, *Doc. Hist.*, p. 351.

excitement and confusion. Joseph Hawley of course heard Whitefield and being very religious as well as easily wrought upon, was undoubtedly aroused to an active part in the events which followed. Perhaps they awoke memories of that earlier phase of the Great Awakening which had had such a tragic climax in the Hawley household.

To a boy from an inland country town like Northampton, association with men from other provinces was a stimulating experience. Yale, to be sure, during the years that Hawley was enrolled had a small student body drawn from what today would seem like a small area but distances then were much greater and knowledge of neighbors much less. A few of the students in this period represented a far different background from Hawley's; some became prominent in the succeeding years, and some were his lifetime associates.

Phinehas Lyman, for instance, who was a tutor throughout the years that Hawley was in Yale, later settled in Suffield and became a prominent lawyer as well as the leading man in the community. Hawley went to Suffield and studied law under him and for a time they were colleagues at the Hampshire County bar. During the French and Indian war Lyman won fame as a general in the Colonial forces; exploiting this reputation, he undertook, about a decade later, an ill-fated colonization project on the lower Mississippi in West Florida.[22]

In the class of 1740 were several men with whom Hawley worked and lived after the days in New Haven. One of these, Adonijah Bidwell, was chaplain of a Connecticut regiment in the expedition against Louisbourg; a similar post was held by Hawley in one of the Massachusetts regiments.[23] Eliphalet Dyer soon entered Connecticut public life, serving for years in the General Assembly. He was at Crown Point in 1755 and when relations became strained with the mother country, he rounded his career

[22] Dexter, *Biog. Sketches*, I, 603.
[23] *Ibid.*, I, 639.

by attending the Stamp Act Congress of 1765, serving in the Continental Congress for many years, and taking an active part on the Connecticut Committee of Safety.[24] A third, and the man whom Hawley came to know the best of all, was John Worthington of Springfield, the "Worthenton" who had helped to raise "prodigious Rought" at the student party in 1738. For years John Worthington and Joseph Hawley were colleagues at the Hampshire County bar. A closer tie resulted from Worthington's marriage to Hawley's cousin, Mary Stoddard.[25]

In the class of 1741 are two names of interest, Jabez Huntington and William Livingston. Huntington combined great activity in the West Indian trade with a generation of service in the General Assembly. When the troubles came he was the most active member of the Connecticut Committee of Safety.[26] Livingston gained a reputation as a New York lawyer and enhanced this position later as a member of the Continental Congress and finally as Governor of New Jersey from 1777 to 1790.[27] One more name attracts attention, that of William Samuel Johnson of the class of 1744. Before becoming the first President of Columbia College in 1787, he had practised law in the Connecticut courts, had been in the Continental Congress and in the Constitutional Convention. From 1789 to 1791 he was a United States Senator and with Oliver Ellsworth helped to frame the famous Judiciary Act of 1789.[28]

Eventually the Yale years ended, and in 1742, Hawley, now a youth of nineteen, was graduated. As he rode slowly northward with the intention of studying theology with Jonathan Edwards, his was a different personality from the one that had entered college three years before. The experience of living away from home, the contacts with men

[24] *Ibid.*, I. 644,
[25] Dexter, *op. cit.*, I. 658.
[26] *Ibid.*, I. 675.
[27] *Ibid.*, I, 682.
[28] *Ibid.*, I, 762.

of other backgrounds than his own, and the intellectual training offered by Yale had broadened the mind of the country boy and opened for him many glimpses into a new and greater world.

Perhaps Hawley studied with his cousin during the year following his graduation from Yale. Certainly in 1742 he became the owner of two works which would have aided him in the study of theology, Bishop Usher's famous *Body of Divinitie* and Dupin's three volume *History of the Church from the Beginning of the World to the Year of Christ 1718*.[29] Possibly he had read Usher's great catechetical presentation while at college, for the work was in the Yale library. Yet there is a certain amount of novelty in the picture of this still raw country youth reading the theological outpourings of that worthy controversialist, the Archbishop of Armagh. Probably they agreed on at least one point—that the Pope was Anti-Christ. But it is even more incongruous to think of Hawley's reading a religious history by a learned Catholic doctor of the Sorbonne, although Dupin's religious views are somewhat subdued and his volumes do contain a vast amount of miscellaneous information about church history.

It must have been about this time that Hawley made a covenant with God to "preach those truths, which I in Conscience think will be for God's honour and Glory, and the Good of Immortall Souls, Not being influenced by the fear of friends or foes. I solemnly vow (if God shall call me to it) to devote my Self to that great work of Striving to win Souls to Jesus Christ; resolving ever to take up Cheerfully the Cross that Christ my master Shall lay before me, and when called to it, Christ Jesus assisting, to Seal the truth of God with my blood, and proclaim it to the world with my latest breathing."[30]

[29] These works with Hawley's autograph and the date are to be found in the library of Miss Clara Hudson of Plainfield, Mass.

[30] This covenant is undated and somewhat mutilated but must have been made about 1743 as it fits only into this period of Hawley's life. Hawley Papers, II, New York Public Library.

FORMATIVE YEARS 19

The next year he was at Cambridge, probably studying theology, but there is no evidence to show he actually attended Harvard College or studied with some minister. Why a young man with the orthodox background and training of Joseph Hawley should have gone to Cambridge, long considered the center of heterodoxy, is difficult to determine, especially since, in 1744, Harvard was in the midst of a great theological controversy. From the days of Increase and Cotton Mather onward Harvard appeared to be straying from the narrow path of orthodoxy. As the eighteenth century progressed the ministers of Boston and the seaboard towns with their opportunities for broader contacts and outlooks had come to preach doctrines that were foreign to strict Calvinism. Some recognized a limited freedom of will; others denied the doctrine of original sin; still others proclaimed universal salvation for all who accepted conversion. Nearly all tended to place increasing weight upon the cultivation of morality as a means to a Christian life, rather than upon morality achieved through a religious experience. Arminians, the orthodox called these men, because some of their ideas resembled those proclaimed more than a century before by the Dutch theologian, Arminius. Upon the heads of the so-called Arminians was heaped untiring abuse and because most of them had attended Harvard, the college was included in the attack by the orthodox. Although the faculty and overseers of Harvard avoided any expression of opinion, circumstances made it appear that they favored the heresies.[31]

George Whitefield had visited Cambridge in 1740, preaching in the church before the students of the college. He excited a good many of them but the faculty remained unmoved and without doubt were opposed to his emotional evangelism. Whitefield in his later sermons and writings continually criticized the religious life at Harvard until in 1744 the President and faculty sponsored the publication of a pamphlet which denounced both his general conduct

[31] J. Quincy, *History of Harvard University*, II, ch. xxii.

and his methods of inducing religious fervor. While even a good many of the orthodox Calvinists disapproved of Whitefield's revivalism, the stand of the Harvard faculty provided further grounds to accuse the college of Arminianism.[32]

Meanwhile, Charles Chauncy, the famous pastor of the First Congregational Church of Boston, was attacking Whitefield's methods and preaching unorthodox doctrines. In 1743 he published a treatise which assailed the belief in original sin and maintained that personal righteousness was necessary for salvation.[33] This was the situation at Boston, but at the other end of the province, Jonathan Edwards, while sensing the dangers of extreme revivalism, had been drawing terrifying pictures not long before of the fate of "sinners in the hands of an angry God," preaching all the tenets of strict Calvinism, original sin and predestination. Hawley had grown up and accepted this theology; yet for some reason when the controversies were still at their height and the stupor after the Great Awakening was spreading religious indifference in the colonies, he journeyed to Cambridge.

It was a significant year for his intellectual development and for his attitude toward the events of later years. For the first time he came in close and intimate contact with that "destructive Error," Arminianism, and being young as well as mentally alert the contact had shocking fascination. Joseph Hawley, as his later life bears witness, possessed a streak of nonconformity and a leaning toward liberalism, both political and religious. With such a temperament and in the Cambridge of 1744 he read "a most Dangerous and Corrupt Book," Experience Mayhew's *Grace Defended in a Modest Plea for an Important Truth.* Experience Mayhew, father of the more famous Jonathan, was in his time a well-known missionary among the Indians

[32] Quincy, *op. cit.*, II, ch. xxii, *passim.*
[33] *Ibid.*, II, 64-65.

## FORMATIVE YEARS

on Martha's Vineyard who, through study and reflection in a search for truth, had turned from orthodox Calvinism to a more moderate position. He believed that man possessed a limited freedom of will and that while salvation was possible only through the grace of God, man should be active in receiving and improving the grace that was offered to him. In his little treatise which Hawley read, Mayhew wrote:

> While you seek to God for his Salvation, rely on his Mercy, & on the Merits of his dear Son; and plead with him his Promises of saving all such as diligently seek him. . . . The Unregenerate may have a Hope and Trust in God, answerable to that Persuasion of his Power and Mercy, which by Means of the glorious Gospel, they have attained to . . . Therefore *seek the Lord while he may be found.* . . . Let nothing discourage you from endeavouring to do so; And while you are thus *drawing nigh unto God, he will draw nigh unto you* James 4,8. Trust in God, he will not fail you.[34]

Hawley was convinced after reading Mayhew's work, although later he wrote that "my Embracing those Wicked Doctrines was owing to the natural Blindness and Pride of my heart, the Wicked and Corrupt nature in which I was born."[35]

But the study of theology and thoughts of the ministry were rudely interrupted. In the spring of 1744 France and Great Britain were at war again—King George's War it was called in the colonies. Massachusetts at the moment possessed in Governor William Shirley "one of the few remarkable Englishmen who occupied office in America" in the eighteenth century.[36] Deciding to raise a force of colonial troops to take Louisbourg, the great French fortress on Cape Breton Island, and supported by public enthusiasm, he raised an army of over three thousand men in

---

[34] Experience Mayhew, *Grace Defended in a Modest Plea for an Important Truth*, p. 207.

[35] Years afterward Hawley described his adventure with Arminianism. A fragment still exists and is among the Hawley Papers.

[36] E. Channing, *History of U. S.*, II, 546.

Massachusetts and secured additional contingents as well as financial aid in the neighboring provinces and colonies. Hampshire County, largely through the work of its indefatigable soldier, Seth Pomeroy, raised for the expedition a company which was attached to the 4th Massachusetts regiment.[37] But it was with the 9th regiment that Joseph Hawley served as chaplain, appointed to pray, preach and read the Holy Scriptures.[38] The expedition was loaded on a fleet of small fishing vessels and sailed on March 24, 1745, from Nantasket Roads. Some weeks later it dropped anchor in the bleak harbor of Canseau, about fifty miles from Louisbourg.

Hawley's experiences with the expedition can only be surmised. His fellow townsman, Seth Pomeroy, was seasick during most of the voyage and suffered from poor food and water throughout the investment of the fortress.[39] Possibly Hawley suffered just as much and like Pomeroy found "that all strong drink . . . was an abomination to him." Sickness was general among the troops, and Hawley must have been busy among them, nursing and praying. On Sundays the chaplains held services and preached; the twenty-two year old chaplain of the Massachusetts 9th could have been no exception. Between times there was the novelty of watching war between white men and the even more remarkable phenomenon of watching inexperienced colonial farmers and mechanics besieging the New World's greatest fortress.

After the surrender of the fortress on the sixteenth of June Hawley lodged within the city. With him at times was Seth Pomeroy who, a few days after the capitulation, recorded in his journal: "I was taken very ill with a flux

[37] Trumbull, *op. cit.*, II, 114.
[38] Hawley Papers, I, 4.
[39] Journal of Seth Pomeroy, pp. 122, 127. This is reproduced entirely in Trumbull's *History of Northampton*, II. Page references are to Trumbull. The original is in the possession of the Forbes Library in Northampton.

## FORMATIVE YEARS 23

and about 2 of the clock in the afternoon cold, agueish, soon after with a terrible headache and fever. I laid myself down upon Mr. Hawley's bed all that afternoon and night and was very sick all night and slept but little."[40] Seth Pomeroy and his men sailed from Louisbourg in July but Hawley stayed longer.[41] Eventually his regiment also sailed for Boston and once more he faced the necessity for beginning his real work in life.

The experiences on the expedition to Louisbourg had been extremely enlightening; here, even more than at New Haven, he had mingled with men from other regions, men from Rhode Island, Connecticut, and New Hampshire as well as from the farther ends of his own province. The roughness of camp life and the absence of religious sentiment among many of his companions may well have disillusioned the young student of theology. This experience, together with his acceptance of Arminianism, apparently turned him from all further thoughts of the ministry. Law appealed to him as an alternative and not long after his return from Louisbourg, he rode southward to Suffield to study law with his former tutor at Yale, Phinehas Lyman.[42]

[40] *Ibid.*, p. 136.
[41] The Reverend Stephen Williams of Longmeadow noted in his diary, on Aug. 6, 1745, that he had prayed with Hawley. This diary is in the possession of the Massachusetts Historical Society.
[42] J. G. Holland, *History of Western Massachusetts*, II. 184.

Chapter III

THE EDWARDS AFFAIR

The theological storm which Joseph Hawley had encountered while at Cambridge soon swept over the province. Northampton did not escape but contributed as its part one of the most extraordinary episodes in the history of colonial religious life, a quarrel between the church and its pastor, Jonathan Edwards, which resulted ultimately in the dismissal from the Northampton church of one of the greatest minds which colonial America produced. The row, for it deserves no more dignified name, arose from a diversity of causes and was continued by as diverse interests until its conclusion. For years it kept the town in ferment, separating old friends and threatening family ties until the noise of it extended beyond the town, beyond the county, and excited wonder among laymen and clergy not only in Massachusetts Bay, but in the more distant colonies and provinces. To understand the controversy, the religious history of Northampton and some of the personal factors involved should be touched upon.

At the time of Hawley's birth in 1723, his grandfather, the Reverend Solomon Stoddard, was rounding out a ministry of nearly sixty years in the Northampton church. Through his intellectual vigor and personal dignity he had attained a leading place among the ministers of the province and had made Northampton truly "a city set upon a hill." More important perhaps was his personal influence with his parishoners. To most of them he had become what his enemies called him, Pope Stoddard, for he had baptized his people, united them in wedlock and spoken the last eulogy over their loved ones. They knew no other religious guide or preceptor and they came to accept his ideas and theological system as the sole truth. This veneration and respect, great in his lifetime, continued to grow with the years after his death—a most important fact. During the years of his pastorate Northampton went through several revivals, notably in 1683, 1712 and 1718. These episodes attracted attention to the church and along with the pastor's friendships and tilts with other religious leaders in the province brought the Northampton church into a prominence which lasted for more than two generations.

One of these debates was with Increase Mather over what came to be known as the "Stoddardean System." At the formation of the Northampton church in the seventeenth century, admission to the sacrament of the Lord's Supper was permitted only to those regarded as regenerate, in other words, to those who upon examination could testify to a religious experience which had converted them into professed Christians. This position was the one generally accepted at the time in all the churches of New England. Stoddard adhered to the principle and practised it for many years, although with growing doubts, until in 1704 he declared in a sermon on the Lord's Supper that in his opinion unconverted persons had a right in the sight of God to come to communion, and that the sacrament was instituted as a means of regeneration, as an incentive towards a religious life, not as an end in itself. This sermon was published three years later and stimulated Increase Mather to an examination and refutation which resulted in the exchange of a series of acrimonious sermons by the two divines. Stoddard's doctrine caused considerable sensation throughout the province, but gradually it was accepted by the Northampton church and most of the churches of Hampshire County.

By the time Jonathan Edwards went to assist his grandfather at Northampton in 1727 the system was firmly rooted and probably no one thought of it as otherwise than permanent. If Edwards had any feeling about the doctrine he made no mention of it and church affairs ran as smoothly after Stoddard's death in 1729 as before. The first outstanding event of Edwards' pastorate was the revival of 1734-1735 when the town "appeared to be full of the appearance of God and it was never so full of love, nor so full of joy, nor yet so full of distress, as it was then." Conversions increased rapidly until almost all the adult population of the town had become church communicants. Visitors heard Edwards preach, caught the infection and spread religious enthusiasm in other parts of the province until the way for the Great Awakening had been well prepared. After Whitefield's visit to Northampton in 1740 another revival began which was more definitely the Great Awakening, lasting until about 1742 when, with emotional exhaustion, it subsided. Meanwhile Edwards by his published accounts of the Northampton revivals, his friendship with Whitefield and his correspondence with the clergy of America and Scotland had achieved wide renown.[1]

But Satan was still present in this wilderness Zion. Almost contemporaneously with the revival, an interest in Arminianism developed among certain groups and spread in a scandalous wave over the region about Northampton. When Edwards preached a series of sermons against the "dangerous" doctrine, he received from many only censure, ridicule and intense opposition. The hostility aroused by this incident never died out while Edwards held the church at Northampton.

One more incident served to set the stage for the controversy and the schism. In 1744 the reaction following the Great Awakening was carrying people into a more natural worldliness when Edwards was informed that licentious books were in the possession of the young people of the town and that they were being used to stimulate obscene conversation among the young at home. Investigations proved that the charges were only too true; immoral,

---

[1] For a general discussion of the state of religion at this time and of the Great Awakening, see H. L. Osgood, *American Colonies in the Eighteenth Century*, Vol. III, Part III, ch. i.

## THE EDWARDS AFFAIR 27

worldly books—what they were no one thought worth recording—were being circulated. Obviously this called for attention from the shepherd of the flock. His first move was to preach on the subject to a startled congregation and then to call a church meeting. At the meeting he held forth on the situation and sought to ascertain the attitude of the church upon the matter. Without hesitation the parishioners voted for an investigation and selected a committee to assist Edwards. At the conclusion of the meeting Edwards asked the committee to meet with him at his home; then with great want of finesse, he read to the church the names of the young people whom he also desired to come to his house. The list contained the names of both witnesses and accused, but as no distinction was made in the reading, the church quickly concluded that all listed were among the reprobate. By this unfortunate slip few families escaped association with the scandal and consternation was general. The thought of investigation suddenly became repugnant to the majority; the innocent protested loudly, and some of the guilty refused to face the committee.[2] Nevertheless, the committee met with the pastor at the appointed time along with some of the youthful miscreants. At Edwards' house the young men involved were assembled in one of the first floor rooms while the girls were in a room above. To the scandal of all, one of the young daredevils placed a ladder against the side of the house, climbed up and looked in the window of the room where the girls were gathered.[3] This was but an incident in the proceedings, which, through the contempt and insolence of the Northampton youth, effectively weakened Edwards' ministry. It was only a minor episode and would have been forgotten if a greater difficulty had not soon arisen.

The Northampton people, particularly the prominent families, were closely interrelated. While kinship did not

[2] S. Dwight, *Life of President Edwards*, pp. 299-300. This biographer reproduces much of the journal which Edwards kept during the period.
[3] Trumbull, *op. cit.*, II, 203.

make necessarily for group solidarity, it tended that way and gave a core about which the uncertain could attach themselves in any period of storm or strife. Blood relationships, moreover, possibly made conflicts more bitter when families did divide on an issue and brother was pitted against brother, cousin against cousin. Though Hawley was a cousin of Jonathan Edwards, it did not prevent his leading the group which opposed the divine. There were other cousins of Jonathan Edwards who also were extremely active against him, and their animosity made the quarrel almost a family feud. The chief of these opponents was Israel Williams of Hatfield, the wealthy "monarch of Hampshire," who had long been a bitter enemy of Edwards. He allied the entire Williams clan against the Northampton minister and may have had some influence on the position assumed by his young Hawley cousin. Thus we arrive at the beginning of the quarrel between the Northampton pastor and his flock.

For some years Edwards had been studying and thinking about the "Stoddardean System" and ultimately he came to believe that the doctrine was wrong. Gradually he disclosed his change of front to his friends, and in 1746 published these new ideas in his *Treatise on Religious Affections.* Even so the church did not realize that a change had taken place because, since the dying down of religious fervor, there had been no applicants for church membership. Late in 1748, however, a young man about to be married went to Edwards and sought admission into the church. The pastor told him of his new views and drew up a profession of faith which the young man refused to take, feeling that any such profession of godliness was unnecessary. When the news of this seeped through the town, it caused great uneasiness; to quiet this feeling and to explain his position, Edwards, in February, 1749, informed the church committee of his new convictions and proposed to preach a series of sermons on the subject.[4] But the majority were

[4] Dwight, *op. cit.*, p. 314.

opposed and suggested rather that he print an essay on his new theological stand. Meanwhile, the town could talk of little else and as Edwards wrote, there was "so great a ferment in the town, that I was satisfied it was not best to preach upon the subject, for the present; and supposed it probable that there would be no opportunity to be heard with any degree of calmness or attention."[5] Before his essay was published he made a written proposal that he should resign his pastorate, if after reading the pamphlet and taking the advice of a council of churches, the Northampton parish should desire it, provided, however, that none of the members should vote on the question unless they had read the essay or heard him preach a defense of his doctrine. Moreover a regular council should be called afterward to approve his resignation. This proposal received scanty consideration from the church committee.[6]

When the pastor's book finally came from the press in mid-August of 1749 the tumult seemed to subside. Yet the town still talked of little else and Joseph Hawley wrote to his brother who was with the troops on the frontier, that "the dispute between him [Edwards] and the people on his late Sentiments engrosses most of the conversation. And I believe that the event will be a separation between him and the people."[7]

Several persons now desired to become members of the church and were willing to accept Edwards' method of admission but the church committee, thoroughly aroused, would not permit it. The pastor suggested that the advice of neighboring ministers should be sought; again the church stubbornly refused to agree. Many people felt that it was time to bring matters to a head; either Edwards should explain his doctrines from the pulpit or a council of ministers and laymen should be called to settle the controversy. Early in October the first definite step was taken by the circulation of a petition among the parishioners for a

[5] *Ibid.*, p. 315.
[6] *Ibid.*, p. 316.
[7] Hawley to Elisha Hawley, Aug. 11, 1749. Hawley Papers I, 16.

precinct meeting "to take into consideration Mr. Edwards' doctrine, with respect to the admission of members into full communion into the church."[8] The meeting was called that very week, on October 19, and after voting down the proposal that Edwards deliver from the pulpit the reasons for his opinions, adjourned for a fortnight. At the adjourned meeting the precinct voted definitely not to accept the new principles.[9] From now on all attempts by Edwards to settle the dispute met with a hostile reception and his proposals were regularly defeated after discussion which only served to rouse passions further. At last, on November 2, the precinct appointed a committee to confer with the minister on a means of settlement.[10]

Here for the first time, although he had undoubtedly played his part from the beginning, Hawley definitely entered the dispute as a member of the precinct committee. He was only twenty-six and as a cousin of Jonathan Edwards might have been expected to remain in the background. But young, already successful, impetuous with the impetuosity of youth, he was soon to throw himself into the midst of Edwards' opponents. Moreover, as an Arminian, his opposition to the pastor was a matter of loyalty to conscience and an act of intellectual honesty.

The committee of which he was a member could reach no agreement with the minister and therefore recommended the calling of a church meeting to decide whether the church should not apply to the nearby clergy for advice and counsel.[11] Edwards immediately took exception, especially

[8] Dwight, *op. cit.*, p. 318. When the townsmen met to consider church affairs, the meeting was called a precinct meeting. Inasmuch as for many years there was only one church in Northampton there was only one precinct and the precinct meetings were actually town meetings convened to consider church matters.

[9] Northampton Town Records, II, 16.

[10] Dwight, *op. cit.*, p. 321.

[11] *Ibid.*, p. 322. It was customary when difficulties arose in a Congregational church to seek the advice of a council of representatives and ministers of other churches. See Williston Walker, *History of Congregational Churches in the U. S.*, p. 247.

## THE EDWARDS AFFAIR 31

to the part which the precinct was playing in the affair, feeling that as a political body, it should not meddle in purely church matters. His position, however, was not sustainable by precedent and was one which in those heated times few were likely to accept. Yet his stand arouses sympathy for it was hardly fair that policies and decisions which vitally affected the pastor should be adopted in a precinct meeting from which he was excluded and then merely ratified in a church meeting which he was forced to call. But there was little of the Christian spirit throughout the entire dispute. As practically all the ministers of the neighboring churches were opposed to Edwards and the advice or counsel which they might be likely to give could be surmised with some degree of accuracy beforehand, the embattled minister insisted that if a council were to be called, both the pastor and the church should have a voice in its selection. This led to further debate and its reference ultimately to a committee of five, among whom was Hawley.[12] Edwards' proposal, while adopted by a majority of this committee, was rejected by the church which now advanced to the position of suspending the sacrament of communion.[13]

Church and committee meetings followed rapidly on one another and ever the gulf between pastor and most of his flock widened. Jonathan Edwards was fighting for every possible advantage if a council should be called, but his enemies were unwilling to yield anything that might jeopardize their case. Finally, on December 12, the church met and after "much earnest talk till after sun-down" voted that a council of five churches, chosen by agreement of the two sides, should be called to decide whether the time was ripe for the calling of a final council to determine whether Edwards should be dismissed from his pastoral office. It was also to decide whether Edwards should be allowed to select some of the members of the final council from outside the county. To manage the church's cause

[12] Dwight, *op. cit.*, p. 325.
[13] *Ibid.*, p. 326.

before the council three men were selected, Ebenezer Pomeroy, Noah Wright and Joseph Hawley.[14] Hawley, however, had been absent when the agents were chosen and being still uncertain of his position, went to Edwards and asked him to inform the church that he declined to serve. On the next Sunday, therefore, after service Edwards announced Hawley's decision to the church, a bombshell that caused many to ask the reason why. According to Edwards, Hawley replied "that his judgments were so different from that of the church, in those points which were referred to the judgment of the Council, that he could not in conscience plead before the Council, for those things on which the church insisted, or to that purpose."[15] Temporarily, at least, Edwards' opponents would have to do without Hawley's support.

The work of the council, which met on December 26, is told by Hawley in a letter to his brother:

The dispute between Mr. Edwards and the Church . . . is very much unsettled tho' people's minds Seem to be calmer than they were before the Council which lately sat here to advise on what course to take under our present difficultys and discord. They advised us to peace charity and moderation, and to attend the ordinance of the Lord's supper, which had been for sum time omitted pursuant to a vote of the Church passed several times. N.B. the votes have been repeated by reason that divers were dissatisfied at the neglect thereof and had prevailed to have the matter reconsidered, which advice of the Council was last Sabbath complied with. They advised for the present to suspend all public agitations of the affair both in Church and precinct. Amongst other things the Church particularly desired the advice of the Council whether (if finally there must be a council to determine whether Mr. Edwards should be dismissed his pastoral office here) such a Council ought any part of them to come from parts out of the County, or without the vicinity or Neighborhood, the resolution

[14] *Ibid.*, p. 339.
[15] *Ibid.*, p. 341

of which point the council deferred to the first tuesday in febry next, to which time they adjourned.[16]

When the council met again the question of Edwards' selecting delegates to the final council from outside the county was hotly debated by the pastor, the church committee and other members of the church. Unfortunately the council was unable to agree, although apparently the general sentiment was for compromise—that the people should not insist on their pastor's selecting all his delegates from Hampshire County but should allow him to select a minority from outside.[17] At this council Edwards saw that his dismissal was imminent and declared that he could not "leave this people without first making trial, Whether my people will hear me give the reasons of my opinion from the pulpit," and sought the council's approval for such a move. This group, however, declined to act, although its members agreed that the minister had a right to preach if he so desired. In order to cause less strife, for Edwards was determined to state his position, he decided to use the Thursday lectures for preaching his doctrines rather than the Sabbath, and in the face of the church's protests, he began on February 15, a series of five lectures.[18] They were thinly attended by members of the Northampton flock but attracted great audiences from the nearby towns. The first lecture coincided with the sitting of the county court which adjourned to hear Mr. Edwards' discourse, much to the wrath of the clerk of court who called the divine "a tyrant, one who lorded it over God's heritage."[19]

During the weeks which followed there was but little progress in the controversy although no signs of its abating. Edwards insisted that he should and would select some members of a final council from beyond the county while

[16] Hawley to Elisha Hawley, Jan. 16, 1750. Hawley Papers, I, 14.
[17] Dwight, *op. cit.*, p. 388.
[18] *Ibid.*, p. 389.
[19] *Ibid.*, p. 390.

the church no less stoutly insisted that he should not. Neither side would yield and neither seemed capable of strengthening its position. About the middle of April Edwards was out of town and during his absence, on April 20, a church meeting was held to decide on the propriety of acting without the minister in calling a council.[20] At this meeting Hawley proposed "That a number of gentlemen, not exceeding seven, ministers or laymen or both, should be mutually chosen from any part of the county, to come, not as sent by their churches, or as an Ecclesiastical Council, but as a number of advisers, to see if they could not devise some way, in which the Pastor and the Church might consist together, notwithstanding their differences in opinion."[21] After a long debate on the question whether this proposal should be laid before the pastor for his approval or before a committee for further consideration, the meeting adopted it and chose a committee of five, Hawley being one, to consider possible amendments or alterations. Though the committee was unable to reach a decision a majority favored Edwards' old plan that he be allowed to choose some members of the council from beyond the county; such a solution was ultimately accepted in a church meeting on April 27. A few days later the church met for a final organization of a council to be held on June 19. At that time Hawley was chosen to be one of the agents for the Northampton church in managing its cause and also to aid in the nomination of the churches which were to be represented on the council.

On the nineteenth of June a council composed of the ministers and delegates of nine churches convened at Northampton; a tenth church selected by Edwards did not send representatives, with the result that Edwards' enemies were in a majority on the council. From outside Hampshire County came delegates from the churches in Sutton

[20] *Ibid.*, p. 396.
[21] *Ibid.*, p. 396.

# THE EDWARDS AFFAIR 35

and Reading.[22] To determine the church's position on Edwards a church meeting was called to vote on the question of dismissal; only twenty-three votes could be found for the minister while over two hundred were against him. Joseph Hawley, the chief spokesman for the church before the council, opposed in a vehement, strenuous way all measures which would prevent immediate dismissal.[23] When the Reverend Mr. Hall of Sutton spoke reminiscently of the former affection and harmony which existed between the church and its pastor, Hawley moved the council to silence and stop him. The pastor's young cousin also read to the council a set of written arguments which contained, as he admitted later, "severe, uncharitable, groundless and slanderous imputations on Mr. Edwards expressed in bitter language." To be sure the younger man had not written these charges himself but he had copied them from another and had agreed to read them to the assembly.[24] After three days of deliberation the council decided by a majority of one that the pastoral relation between Edwards and the Northampton church should be dissolved, and "recommending the Rev. Mr. Edwards, and the church in Northampton, to the grace of God," adjourned. The minority entered a protest against the desire for haste and the zeal for separation which dominated the Northampton people, but the protest was unavailing; the Northampton pastorate of Jonathan Edwards was ended.

Hawley's part in the controversy is told in a letter which Edwards wrote to one of his Scottish correspondents. "The people in managing this affair on their side," he wrote in part, "have made chief use of a young gentleman of liberal education and notable abilities, and a fluent speaker, of about seven or eight and twenty years of age, my grandfather Stoddard's grandson, being my mother's sister's son, a man of lax principles in religion, falling in, in

[22] *Ibid.*, p. 398-99.
[23] *Ibid.*, p. 410-12.
[24] *Ibid.*, p. 423.

some essential things, with Arminians, and is very open and bold in it. He was improved as one of the agents of the church, and was their chief spokesman before the council. He very strenuously urged before the council the necessity of an immediate separation."[25] Edwards feared the infleuence of Hawley's Arminianism and in this same letter wrote:

There seems to be the utmost danger, that the younger generation will be carried away with Arminianism, as with a flood. The young gentleman I spoke of, is high in their esteem, and is become the most leading man in town; and is very bold in declaiming and disputing for his opinions; and we have none able to confront and withstand him in dispute; and some of the young people already show a disposition to fall in with his notions, and it is not likely that the people will obtain any young gentleman with Calvinistic sentiments to settle with them in the ministry, who will have courage and ability to make head against him.[26]

In the heat of the moment Edwards perhaps exaggerated Hawley's influence, particularly in the matter of religion, but certainly from this time until his death a generation later, Joseph Hawley was the leading and outstanding figure in Northampton.

Several years after Edwards' dismissal from the Northampton church, he was in communication with Hawley and took occasion to express in no uncertain terms his opinion of his younger cousin's conduct during the affair:

I think, [wrote Edwards] you made your Self greatly guilty in the sight of God, in the Part you acted in this affair; becoming especially the latter Part of it, very much their Leader in it; & much from your own forwardness, putting your Self forward as it were, as tho fond of intermeddling & Helping, which was less becoming, considering your youth, and considering your Relation to me. Your forwardness especially appeared on this occasion, that after you were chosen as one of a committee to plead their

[25] Trumbull, *op. cit.*, II, 230.
[26] Edwards to Reverend Mr. Erskine, July 5, 1750. Quoted in Dwight *op. cit.*, p. 410-11.

cause before Council, you came to me and desired .... to excuse yourself and were excused. But yet when this matter came to be pleaded before the Council, you, (I think very inconsistently) thrust yourself Forward and pleaded the cause with much Earnestness .... Tis manifest that what you did in the affair, from Time to Time, not only helped the People to gain their End in dismissing me but much encouraged and promoted the Spirit with which it was done; your Confidence, magisterial, vehement manner had a natural & direct tendency to it.[27]

When passions had cooled, Hawley began to be ashamed of his part in the controversy and wrote to Edwards, who was then at Stockbridge, for judgment and possible pardon. In his final letter he apologized in most humble terms for what he had done, admitting that what he had said "was Irreverent immodest derisive magisterial & savouring of haughtiness & levity and Such as very ill became me when arguing with you Sr who was so much my Superior in age Station and accomplishments, and who deserved from me great respect and defference for which I humbly and sincerely ask your forgiveness, and am very Sorry, not only for that it was disrespectful to you Sr, but also a very ill Example to others and a tendency to abate the respect and reverence which the bystanders ought to have maintained and probably had an Influence upon the hearers towards prompting them to a disrespectful and irreverent treatment of you afterwards."[28]

Ten years after the proceedings when Edwards was in his grave and people had begun to forget the affair, Hawley wrote to the Reverend Mr. Hall of Sutton, one of the members of the council which sat on Edwards' case, a long letter of contrition and confession, a letter which soon found the light through publication in one of the Boston papers. Here he greatly blamed himself for his part in the affair and asked humbly and earnestly the forgiveness of God, the forgiveness of the relatives and near friends of

[27] J. Edwards to J. Hawley, Nov. 18, 1754. Hawley Papers, I, 35.
[28] J. Hawley to J. Edwards, Jan. 11, 1755. Hawley Papers, I, 36.

Mr. Edwards, of those called Edwards' adherents, of the members of the ecclesiastical councils, and of all Christian peoples who had any knowledge of what had happened.[29] The eating of humble pie could not have been easy although it gave Hawley great reputation for a sense of justice and right and the historian of the province wrote, "This ingenuous confession raised his character more than his intemperate conduct had lessened it."[30]

But all this came after the storm. On July 1, 1750, Jonathan Edwards preached his farewell sermon to the Northampton church, exhorting them to maintain family order, to avoid contention, to watch against Arminianism, to give themselves to prayer and to take great care in the settlement of a minister among them. Then, invoking the blessing of God upon this wayward flock, he surrendered his pastorate.[31]

Actually it was not Edwards' last sermon in the town, for during the following months he frequently preached in the church as the committee found it difficult to secure anyone else and was forced to turn, however reluctantly, to the dismissed pastor.[32] Gradually the town became very uneasy that he should continue to preach before the people, and voted at a precinct meeting in November, "That it was not agreeable to their minds that he should preach among them."[33] But among his old parishioners were many good friends who insisted that it was his duty to stay with them, even if it meant the organization of another church in Northampton. Apparently Edwards felt that this action would only perpetuate the discord but at last he yielded so far as to consent to seek advice from another council, and accordingly one met on May 15, 1751. It caused a tumult in the town; a church meeting was hur-

[29] J. Hawley to Hall, May 9, 1760.   Hawley Papers, I.
[30] T. Hutchinson, *History of Massachusetts Bay*, III, 296.
[31] Dwight, *op. cit.*, pp. 648-65.
[32] *Ibid.*, p. 416.
[33] *Ibid.*, p. 418.

riedly called and a committee was appointed to draw up a remonstrance to the council. On this committee was the leader in the first stages of the dispute, Hawley, and he had a large share both in drawing up the remonstrance and in securing its adoption. Later, he admitted that the document was "interlarded with unchristian bitterness, sarcastical and unmannerly insinuations. It contained divers direct grevious, and criminal charges and allegations against Mr. Edwards, which," as he wrote, "I have since good reason to suppose, were all founded on jealous and uncharitable mistakes, and so, were really gross slanders; also many heavy and reproachful charges upon divers of Mr. Edwards' adherents, and some severe censures of them all indiscriminately, all of which, if not wholly false and groundless, were altogether unnecessary, and therefore highly criminal."[34] The council immediately asked the committee to come before it and prove the charges but this, largely through Hawley's influence, the committee refused to do. The church, too, was invited to a friendly conference with the council, but this likewise and probably through Hawley's consistent opposition was declined.[35] Finally the council recommended that Edwards accept an invitation which he had been considering to go to Stockbridge; thus the incident was closed. In October, he moved his family from the town where he had known so much joy and sorrow, and began his new work among the whites and Indians at Stockbridge.

Meanwhile the church in Northampton had been seeking a new pastor without much success. Few men were willing to accept a call when the memory of the treatment meted out to Edwards was still fresh and during the first few months, as has been said, Edwards filled the pulpit when other supplies could not be found. The whole situation is set forth in a letter which Hawley wrote to his brother. "We have no Candidate here," he wrote, "nor

[34] Hawley to Hall, May 9, 1760. Hawley Papers, I.
[35] *Loc. cit.*

have we ever had any yet. Mr. Frink preached with us two months, to good satisfaction but he was not with us on probation. Capt. Wright was sent to the Jerseys for a Mr. Arthur, but he was sick and died soon. Mr. Wright then obtained through Prest. Burr of New Jersey College knowledge of Mr. Farrand, a graduate last commencement. He was highly recommended by President Burr. . . . Our estate is very melancholy whoever is in the mistake either Mr. Edwards or the people that surely our loss of him and the difficulty we meet in endeavoring for a Candidate are tokens of the great displeasure of the almighty. May God be merciful unto us."[36]

The Mr. Farrand whom Hawley mentions preached satisfactorily for several months in the Northampton church and in the spring of 1752 was invited to settle. For some reason, possibly because the vote was not unanimous, he declined the call and the Northampton flock was still without a shepherd.[37] Nor did the months bring any improvement; quarrels appeared among the parishioners and no one could be found to preach. As Edwards wrote:

The people of Northampton are in sorrowful circumstances, are still destitute of a minister, and have met with a long series of disappointments, in their attempts for a resettlement of the ministry among them. My opposers have had warm contentions among them. Of late, they have been wholly destitute of any body, to preach steadily among them. They sometimes meet to read and pray among themselves, and at other times set travellers or transient persons to preach, that are hardly fit to be employed.[38]

According to tradition when one of those who were hardly fit, a transient named Jones, occupied the pulpit he made such a botch of the service that Hawley turned him out of the pulpit and finished the service himself.[39]

[36] Hawley to Elisha Hawley, March 11, 1751. Hawley Papers, I, 18.
[37] Trumbull, *op. cit.*, II, 237.
[38] Dwight, *op. cit.*, p. 518.
[39] Trumbull, *op. cit.*, II, 238.

At last conditions began to improve; in 1753 the Reverend John Hooker was invited to settle, and on the fifth of December, 1753, was ordained. During the quarter century of Hooker's pastorate he became one of Joseph Hawley's most intimate friends. Possibly in part because of this friendship Hawley eventually abandoned Arminianism and became a more safely orthodox member of the First Church of Northampton.

CHAPTER IV

ATTORNEY AND BARRISTER

When the years with Phinehas Lyman were over, Hawley came home to Northampton to begin the practice of law among his own people. Study and observation had already made him familiar with the judicial system of Massachusetts Bay, a system established and regulated by a series of acts passed in 1692 and 1699. Under them a kind of hierarchy had been set up although the term is scarcely appropriate to the simple society of the time. More than three generations had served to give the system stability and fixity, and it was to remain essentially unchanged until overwhelmed by the rising tide of revolution in 1774. Like most colonial institutions it was English in inspiration and only altered where necessary to meet American conditions and needs.

At the base of this judicial hierarchy were the justices of the peace and their courts with jurisdiction in all concerns of debts, trespasses, and other matters in which the total sum involved did not exceed forty shillings. To carry these powers into effect the justices issued processes against defendants a week before the holding of court. They issued warrants and executions of distress under their judgement, drew up deeds and all other legal documents of a semi-private nature. Furthermore, they could and did commit beggars and disorderly persons to the workhouse or imposed fines upon them of not more than twenty shillings.[1] In short a justice of the peace was literally that; his function was to settle easily and quickly the petty squabbles of community life.

[1] E. Washburn, *Judicial History of Massachusetts*, pp. 170-71.

## ATTORNEY AND BARRISTER 43

All criminal cases were heard by the Court of General Sessions of the Peace and in certain instances, appeals from the decisions of the justices of the peace. Like the Court of Common Pleas, this was also a county court and like the former also had trial by jury. Its quarterly sittings with a bench of the justices of the peace coincided with the sittings of the Court of Common Pleas. Some of its functions, however, seem to have been hardly judicial, because actually the Court of General Sessions was a kind of governing body. It had complete financial control of the county, assessing the towns and spending the income from these assessments; it controlled and managed all jails or houses of correction, granted licenses to innholders, liquor retailers and ferrymen. Under its jurisdiction also were the locating and establishing of county highways, a highly important power in a new country.[2]

If an individual believed that he had not received his due at the hands of the justices of the peace, he could appeal to the Court of Common Pleas and obtain a jury trial. This was a county court sitting quarterly with a bench of four judges. Its jurisdiction extended to all civil actions triable at common law as well as to the hearing of appeals from the decisions of the justices of the peace.[3]

The highest tribunal of the province, a court which met annually in each county, was the Superior Court of Judicature. On its bench sat the chief justice of the province and four associates, hearing all appeals from the lower courts and exercising original as well as concurrent jurisdiction in all matters of freehold in which the amount involved was £10 or more. In short, it was a court of assize and general gaol delivery, exercising jurisdiction over all actions, real, personal, or mixed. The judges of the court who in the days of the province could be removed by the governor and council established all necessary rules and orders governing practice in their courts.[4]

[2] Washburn, *op. cit.*, pp. 169-70.
[3] *Ibid.*, p. 168.   [4] *Ibid.*, p. 152.

A sitting of the Superior Court was an occasion of considerable importance and a time of social festivity as well. At such times the shire town was certain to be thronged with spectators and lawyers and their clients. When the justices of the court approached the shire town, they were met on the outskirts by the high sheriff of the county and his posse, composed in this instance of distinguished citizens. Thus escorted, they rode into town through the gaping populace until they reached their lodgings in the best tavern or in the home of some local dignitary. But it was in the actual sitting of the court that the majesty of the law was best displayed. Particularly was this true in the latter years of the royal government when Thomas Hutchinson was chief justice. At the sessions, the judges, resplendent in scarlet robes, broad bands and great judicial wigs, sat upon a platform raised above the level of the courtroom. Before them pled the barristers in black gowns, bands, and tye-wigs, and the attorneys in suits of simple black.[5] It was an impressive scene not soon to be forgotten.[6]

By the middle of the eighteenth century the position of the bar throughout the province was improving. For many years the profession had been in ill repute as a result of the poor training or lack of training of its members and their constant use of trifling technicalities in pleas and prosecutions. The extremely haughty and distant attitude of the judges towards attorneys and clients also gave the bar a bad reputation with the average man. A change came about largely as the result of regulations drawn up by the bar of Suffolk County which were soon copied throughout the province. They prescribed three years of study in

[5] *Ibid.*, pp. 162-63. The painting by Robert Reid in the Massachusetts State House, representing James Otis pleading against the writs of assistance, reproduces a sitting of the Superior Court. See also C. F. Adams, *Works of J. Adams*, II, 133; X, 2-33.

[6] George Bliss, *Address to the Hampshire County Bar*, p. 31. Bliss said: "I saw the court when a boy, and making all due allowance for the effect upon the mind of a child, I feel confident that no earthly tribunal could inspire greater reverence than its appearance did on my mind."

## ATTORNEY AND BARRISTER 45

the law before admission to the bar as an attorney.[7] Only after seven years' probation could an attorney become a barrister, but the period included the three years of study for admission to the bar, two years of practice in the inferior court, and two years of practice as an attorney in the higher court.[8] Actually, however, practice before the Superior Court was permitted only after three years of practice in the lower court and frequently a man practiced as an attorney many years more than the required seven before becoming a barrister.[9] During this period when admission to the bar was being better regulated, procedure was freed from many irritating technicalities, although the manner of the court towards those appearing before it continued to be distant and severe.[10]

The training lawyers received varied considerably and today would seem superficial. The use of the common law was the rule and included on rare occasions even the benefit of clergy, for this was the basis of John Adams' defense of the soldiers involved in the Boston Massacre.[11] Few law books were known in the province and these related to "black letter" law; Bracton, Britton, Fleta and Glanville were perhaps the mediaeval works best known.[12] Although Blackstone's *Commentaries* did not come into general use until about 1770, many a lawyer's meagre library included, besides the mediaeval authorities, Bacon's *Abridgment*, the works of Coke, Littleton, Hale, Gilbert, Rastell and Fitzherbert.[13]

The manner of John Adams' admission to the bar was probably typical of the experience many aspiring lawyers

[7] *Ibid.*, p. 27.
[8] H. R. Bailey, *Attorneys and Their Admission to the Bar in Massachusetts*, p. 20.
[9] C. F. Adams, *Works of John Adams*, II, 133-97.
[10] Washburn, *op. cit.*, p. 198.
[11] *Ibid.*, p. 189. For a more recent and able discussion of colonial law in general, see R. B. Morris, *Studies in the History of American Law*.
[12] *Works of J. Adams*, II, 49.
[13] Bliss, *op. cit.*, pp. 67-68.

went through. Jeremiah Gridley, one of the leaders of the bar in the middle of the eighteenth century, served as Adams' guide and patron. To him fell the rôle of securing the bar's approval of the young neophyte and then of recommending him to the court. Gridley gave Adams several works to read that would serve as a guide in study; among them were Lord Hale's advice to a student of the common law, Lord Reeve's advice, a letter on the method of studying the common law from Dr. Dickens, Regius Professor of Law at the University of Cambridge, and a valuable letter on the study of admiralty law by Lightfoot, Judge of the Admiralty in Rhode Island. Gridley pointed out to Adams that in Massachusetts a lawyer "must study common law, and civil law, and natural law, and admiralty law; and must do the duty of a counsellor, a lawyer, an attorney, a solicitor and even of a scrivener." His parting advice was "to pursue the study of the law, rather than the gain of it; pursue the gain of it enough to keep out of the briers, but give your main attention to the study of it." After this fatherly session, the candidate was introduced to the leaders of the bar and recommended for admission. Soon afterwards, he took the oath and then invited his new associates to a nearby tavern where a bowl of punch cemented the relationship.[14]

Exactly when Joseph Hawley was admitted to the bar is not certain. His name first appears in the records of the Court of Common Pleas for Hampshire County at its May sitting in 1749.[15] As he could not have finished the study of law much earlier, this must be near the date of his admission to practice. In November of that year he was commissioned a justice of the peace; it was the beginning of a quarter of a century in legal practice and nearly forty years in the post of justice of the peace.[16] Not until the

[14] *Works of J. Adams*, II, 46-49.
[15] Records of the Court of Common Pleas, Hampshire County, 1749, p. 52. Hereinafter cited as Common Pleas.
[16] Records of the Court of General Sessions of the Peace, Hampshire County, 1749, p. 75. Hereinafter cited as General Sessions.

August sitting of the Superior Court in Suffolk County in 1762 was he allowed to appear in the gown of a barrister at the same time as James Otis, Richard Dana, John Worthington, Oxenbridge Thacher, Robert Auchmuty and others.[17] With his colleagues in Hampshire County, Hawley is said to have secured the adoption of rules regulating admission to the bar and ending the arbitrariness and illiberality which had often crushed justice by the weight of technicalities. By these and other measures he aided in making the Hampshire bar "one of the most respectable, not to say brilliant, in the colony."[18]

Associated with him were other men of ability and reputation. For some years his old teacher, Phinehas Lyman of Suffield, was a colleague and leader in the profession. But soon after the final settlement of the Massachusetts-Connecticut boundary in 1749, when Suffield was placed outside Massachusetts, Lyman disappeared from Hampshire circles. As the years rolled by, John Worthington was Hawley's constant associate. Lighter in temperament, quicker mentally than Hawley, and generally on the opposing side in suits, he nevertheless allied himself with the latter to improve and maintain the standards of the Hampshire bar. Together they were its leaders.[19] Another of Hawley's associates was his cousin, Israel Williams of Hatfield, who for many years was a justice of the peace. They were never on very good terms and eventually became bitter political enemies. Theodore Sedgwick of Great Barrington and Simeon Strong of Amherst, both of whom at the end of the century were associate justices in the Supreme Court of the new Massachusetts government, were also members of the circle.

At the sessions of the Superior Court, Hawley met other attorneys and barristers. One of them was James Sullivan who served Massachusetts many years as attorney-general

[17] Records of the Superior Court of Judicature, 1762, p. 40.
[18] J. G. Holland, *History of Western Massachusetts*, I, 183-85.
[19] Bliss, *op. cit.*, p. 27.

and in his last years as governor. He was younger than Hawley and had great respect for the older man who apparently influenced him considerably. Whenever he practiced in Hampshire County, he stayed with the Hawleys at their Northampton home in Pudding Lane.[20] Another prominent attorney whom Hawley met through the Superior Court was John Adams. Adams many years later described their meeting: "This week, 1768, I attended Superior Court at Worcester, and the next week proceeded to Springfield, in the county of Hampshire, where I was accidentally engaged in a case between a negro and his master, which was argued by me, I know not how; but it seems it was in such a manner as engaged the attention of Major Hawley, and introduced an acquaintance which was soon after strengthened into friendship that continued till his death."[21]

Hawley's reputation as a lawyer rested on several things; his profound knowledge of "black letter" law, his dignity and oratorical power, and his unusual scrupulousness. The sort of training he had received with Phinehas Lyman can only be surmised, but presumably it had been in old English works. Certainly his reputation was one of being deeply versed in the old forms of English practice.[22] Tradition has made him conversant with Bracton, Fleta and Rastell.[23] Years afterwards, when his reputation was made, he purchased the law library of Phinehas Lyman which contained a valuable collection of ancient English authors.[24] He knew Lord Hale and cited him liberally in a long article written for the Boston *Evening Post* in

[20] T. C. Amory, *Life of Sullivan*, I, 94. After Hawley's death, Sullivan gave the town of Boston land for a highway on condition that it be named for his old friend. So visitors to Boston will find there a Hawley Street today.

[21] *Works of J. Adams*, II, 213.

[22] Holland, *op. cit.*, I, 185.

[23] Bliss, *op. cit.*, p. 38.

[24] S. Clark, *Northampton Antiquities*, p. 172.

## ATTORNEY AND BARRISTER 49

1768.[25] Coke on Littleton, which he purchased in 1758 for £5/13/4, was familiar to him of course and was cited along with Blackstone in an argument written about 1770 on the question, "Are the Justices of the Superior Court removable at Pleasure or for just Cause only."[26] Moreover in his commonplace book, he wrote an explanation of a passage in Blackstone's third volume which was not so "clear and obvious" as others.[27]

All witnesses agree on Hawley's gravity and solemnity. He was impressive in speech and forceful in argument.[28] Juries had great confidence in his assertions and were doubtlessly swayed by his oratorical powers.[29] In his grave, austere way he possessed a powerful eloquence; as we shall see, it thrilled the Massachusetts House of Representatives and it could scarcely have failed to have impressed country juries. Timothy Dwight who grew up in Northampton wrote of him: "Many men have spoken with more elegance and grace—I never heard one speak with more force."[30] More important in a simply organized community than knowledge and eloquence was a reputation for integrity. In time it became proverbial that Joseph Hawley would never engage in a case in which his client's cause was not on the side of justice, and similarly, he would drop a case if it became apparent that he was on the wrong side.[31] His strict honesty and conscientiousness were recognized by those who disagreed with him politically; even Thomas Hutchinson recorded that "some instances have been mentioned of singular scrupulosity, and of his refusing and returning fees when they appeared

[25] Boston *Evening Post*, Jan. 25, 1768.
[26] Hawley Papers, I, 87. In the Hawley Papers also there is a note from some merchant to Hawley, written in 1758, which quotes to him the price of Coke.
[27] "Commonplace Book," Hawley Papers, II.
[28] Washburn, *op. cit.*, p. 227.
[27] Bliss, *op. cit.*, p. 37.
[30] T. Dwight, *Travels*, I, 300.
[31] Holland, *op. cit.*, I, 185.

## 50 ATTORNEY AND BARRISTER

to him greater than the cause deserved."[32] If his client chanced to be a widow or orphan he never took a fee, and for general advice charged as little as twelve and a half cents. In one instance, after spending an entire afternoon giving an opinion on a land case, Hawley charged a fee of only two pistareens (about twenty cents).[33] Small wonder that his extensive practice brought little to his pocket.

Hawley's practice was for the most part confined to Hampshire County, but it must be remembered that during nearly half his career in law, this county included all western Massachusetts, the area now divided into the four counties of Berkshire, Franklin, Hampshire and Hampden. After the organization of Berkshire County in 1761 Hawley seldom appeared in its courts; he had all the practice he could attend to in Hampshire alone. While Northampton was designated as the county seat, the sittings of the inferior courts alternated between the county seat and Springfield.[34] In March and November the courts sat at Northampton, in May and August at Springfield. Throughout most of its history, the Superior Court sat at Springfield every September, but from 1771 to 1774, owing in part to Hawley's influence, an additional term was held at Northampton.[35] During most of these years the court at Northampton met in a hip-roofed structure that served also as a place for town meetings. At the end of its one room, opposite the door, the judges sat upon a raised platform, while the spectators were seated facing the central aisle. This court house had seemed very grand at its completion in 1737, but a generation of use and New England weather brought about such dilapidation that a new building was required in 1767.[36] Hawley, who was anxious that the court house should continue to stand on Meeting-house Hill,

[32] Hutchinson, *op. cit.*, III, 296.
[33] Notes of George Bancroft, Hawley Papers, I.
[34] Bliss, *op. cit.*, p. 16.
[35] Trumbull, *op. cit.*, II, 331.
[36] *Centennial Gazette*, Northampton, 1876, p. 3.

## ATTORNEY AND BARRISTER 51

raised funds by subscription to purchase the needed land. Such an inducement insured the location of the new building on the slope where Hampshire County court houses have stood from that day to this.

An analysis of Hawley's practice is not easy. It reflected the simple yet diversified social and economic life of its time and place, combining squires and yeomen, merchants and mechanics in hundreds of actions for debt or trespass. The vast majority of the causes in which he was attorney were simple suits for the collection of debts; yet many drew him into extremely tangled skeins which were unraveled with only the greatest difficulty. Next in number to actions for debt were issues concerned with realty holdings. In a country where land titles and boundaries frequently were not recorded or not carefully surveyed, such suits were to be expected. Furthermore, the prevailing land speculation added to the confusion of titles, especially when the heirs of a land speculator investigated the actual holdings which were supposed to be theirs. Actions for violations of contract were numerous, and it is perhaps in them that some phases of economic life are most clearly shown. While Hawley did not indulge generally in what might be termed criminal practice, he handled a good many cases of "trespass" which fell outside questions of contract into the category of torts.

Quite naturally as a justice of the Court of General Sessions he seldom appeared before the court in the rôle of attorney but occasionally the records show his acting in some criminal suit or as the agent for Northampton in county matters. Infrequently he acted in what might be termed a freak suit for damages as compensation for personal injuries. Before the Superior Court his practice, so far as can be determined, consisted exclusively of appeals taken from the lower courts, and therefore were of the same general character as before the county tribunals.

For the most part Hawley's clients were obscure; sometimes important in their own communities but, more often than not, merely average citizens of whom nothing is known beyond their designation in the records as "miller," "yeoman," or "wheelwright." One of the most noted of Hawley's clients was the Boston merchant, Thomas Hancock, the uncle of the more famous John, who in his day was one of the leading merchants in the province. Exactly when Hawley began to act for him in western Massachusetts is unknown but it was sometime before 1763, for in a letter to Hancock in that year Hawley refers to having been employed previously in the management of Hancock's suits.[37] After the death of Thomas Hancock in 1764, Hawley served his heir, John, in what few suits the latter had occasion to enter in the Hampshire courts.[38]

John Rowe, another well-known Boston merchant was also a client of Hawley's and employed him to collect debts owed to the Rowe house in the towns of Hawley's county. While it may be only a coincidence, Hawley was not employed until he had become prominent in the political life of the province.[39] Their relations were on a social footing and when Hawley was in Boston, he dined at John Rowe's and drank his Madeira.[40] In 1766 Lady Mary Pepperell of Kittery and Benjamin Greenleaf of Newburyport, executors of the estate of Sir William Pepperell, employed Hawley in a successful action for the collection of debts in Hampshire County.[41]

It was seldom, however, that Hawley appeared for such prominent persons. More often he acted for the less known of Boston. During 1767-1768 he was prosecuting for Jane Eustice, a milliner of Boston, in a plea of trespass against one Benoni Danks of Chignecto, Nova Scotia, a

[37] Hawley to T. Hancock, Feb. 23, 1763. Washburn Manuscripts, XXII, 64. Mass. Hist. Soc.
[38] Common Pleas, 1766, p. 157; 1767, p. 109; 1771, p. 75.
[39] *Ibid.*, 1769, p. 432, 435; 1770, p. 492; 1771, p. 75.
[40] Diary of John Rowe. Extracts printed in *Mass. Hist. Soc. Pro.*, X, 83.
[41] Common Pleas, 1766, p. 218.

case which he eventually won for the lady.[42] On another occasion he appeared for Henry Leddel, the Boston merchant, in a plea of debt and won the case through default.[43] Frequently he was attorney for his fellow townsmen, most of whom time has forgotten. His friend and colleague, Seth Pomeroy, retained him in various actions for debt, and so did his erstwhile pupil, Caleb Strong.[44] Then finally he was generally the agent for the town of Northampton in whatever suits it might enter or be forced to defend.

Quite naturally most of Hawley's clients were drawn from the towns and the villages of far-spreading Hampshire County, but not all. We have seen that he acted for some of the Boston merchants; he also had clients in several of the eastern towns—Chelsea, Braintree, and Scituate at least. In a long series of actions Abraham Fonda, a merchant in Claverack, Albany County [now Columbia County], Province of New York, employed Hawley, as did others in the region. Litigants in northern Connecticut recognized his ability and did not hesitate to entrust their suits to his hands. Probably the following letter from one John Merritt of Providence, Rhode Island, was typical of many that Hawley received during the years of his practice:

.... Expecting Ere now to have had the pleasure of hearing from you upon Mr. Auchmuty's Delivery to you at Springfield a letter & power of attorney From me to sue me into possession of the Tract of Land in Ware River precinct (That Gent. gave you a deed of) From Henry Paget to me: I Say Depending on notice from you, That you had Executed the same, made me all the while not write you. At last a month ago I sent to Mr. Paget to know if he had heard from you & this week have his ans. that he has not; but, That he would write you. Now Sir, Tho I hope The same is gon Thro The Court & Execution is Served, that I may Forthwith Endeavour The sale of it; yet for fear Should it not be done, I afresh Trouble you,

[42] *Ibid.*, 1767, p. 64; 1768, p. 266.
[43] *Ibid.*, 1768, p. 291.
[44] *Ibid.*, 1771, pp. 74, 79.

begging you, if not done, that you'll not fail performing the Needful at the next Inferiour Court coming on at the place. For Tho I again & again applied to Mr. Paget to redeem the Land, by paying me my money, nay offered to make abatement, yet it is all To no purpose. For he Thinks The Land worth more Than the debt, & therefore I Still give him leave to Trye, and shall do so a little after I am in possession, being no way Inclined to Take advantage of him but I am afraid If I loose the present time for sale of it—purchasers will go Further inland on our Conquests, & I shall not be able for some time after to sell it at all— and I Am Infirm & in years & Therefore Shall be glad to see an Issue of it—I asked him if he had ordered any plea to be made against my action, & he ans'r me No. Nor do I Suppose There is—May I beg the favor of an ans'r Forthwith, sending to your Friend at Boston with directions to put it into the post house There. . . . The Charge attending This affair please to Let me know & I will pay it to your order in Boston. . . .[45]

During his quarter of a century of practice, Hawley must have had a good many students reading law under his direction; precisely how many or who they were we can only surmise, but two of them became conspicuous in the next generation. One was Levi Lincoln of Worcester, the future attorney-general in the cabinet of Thomas Jefferson.[46] He was a student in the last days of the royal government when Thomas Jefferson was still unknown and independence was still in the future. The other was Caleb Strong, a Northampton youth who was to be a member of the Constitutional Convention of 1787, United States senator, ten times a governor of Massachusetts and finally the president of the Hartford Convention.[47] There were others, of course, among them, Hawley's adopted son, Joseph Clarke, who were village boys and became village lawyers, leavening their own circles but lost to the story of the greater society.

[45] John Merritt to Hawley, Dec. 21, 1760. Hawley Papers, II.
[46] *Mass. Hist. Soc. Pro.*, Ser. I, Vol. XIII, p. 207.
[47] *Ibid.*, Ser. I, Vol. I, pp. 293-94.

ATTORNEY AND BARRISTER 55

To indicate the nature of Hawley's practice more specifically, some of his cases may well be outlined. As already noted, the most numerous were rather simple actions for debt. Such was a suit by one Joseph Billings of Belchertown against Sampson Wood of the same village. For various articles which the clerk of the court did not see fit to enumerate, Wood owed Billings £14/13/16 and besides, another debt for £14/13/6. When this case came before the Court of Common Pleas at Springfield in May, 1762, Hawley appeared for Billings while John Worthington defended Wood. The latter successfully sustained the plea that he had never owed anything to Billings in the manner and form alleged, and secured costs of court. Hawley then appealed to the Superior Court of Judicature.[48] Apparently the case was settled later out of court, for when it was called at the September sitting in 1763, neither party appeared.[49] Scores of such cases can be found, some slightly more involved, some less, but all essentially the same.

The pleas used in defense of some cases are worth noting. In the case of Spooner vs. Burt, Hawley, the attorney for the defendant, pleaded that the plaintiff's writ was bad because it designated Burt as a yeoman when he was really a gentleman. The court, however, held that this plea was insufficient, although it returned a verdict for Burt when his attorney maintained that the defendant's bond had never been given in the manner and form alleged in the writ.[50] In another case, that of McLean vs. Burbank, the defendant was sued for £127 (New York currency) which he was alleged to owe by reason of a bond given to McLean. Hawley, the attorney for the defense, pleaded that the bond was illegal because it charged the defendant, who was a resident of Suffield, Connecticut, more than six per cent interest, a rate contrary to Connecticut

[48] Common Pleas, 1762, p. 308.
[49] Superior Court of Judicature, 1763, p. 153.
[50] Common Pleas, 1762, p. 33.

law. Nevertheless the court decided against Burbank.[51] When the case of Gager vs. Mattoon, an action for debt, was heard in 1760, Hawley for the defendant sought an abatement of the plaintiff's writ as the name upon it was different from that in the bond alleged to have been given by Mattoon to Gager. The abatement was denied, although the court awarded the plaintiff a verdict of two pence.[52]

Throughout the years of his practice, Hawley was involved in cases concerning land titles. They were of two kinds, those in which the plaintiffs sued for damages because they had been sold land with a bad title, and those in which the plaintiffs sued to regain possession of real estate which in some manner they had lost. The former is illustrated by the case of Wood *et al.* vs. Hutchinson. In 1738 or thereabouts, one Edward Hutchinson of Milton had sold to the plaintiffs for £800 a tract of land on the Chicopee river in Hampshire County. This title was supposed to be in fee simple but in 1750 one Benjamin Morgan with an apparently better title took possession of part of the land. Hutchinson made no defense of the title, and the plaintiffs therefore employed Hawley to act for them in recovering damages of £550. The suit in the inferior court, brought in a plea of covenant broken, was prosecuted unsuccessfully, and although appealed was apparently never acted upon further.[53] Of a different nature was the suit of John Still Winthrop against James Blake. Winthrop was seeking the ejectment of Blake from a tract of 120 acres in South Brimfield which, he maintained, was part of his inheritance, although Blake had long been in actual possession. Here, as so often, Worthington opposed Hawley before the court, but Hawley, appearing for the defendant, won the cause and secured costs of court for his client.[54]

[51] *Ibid.*, 1761, p. 225.
[52] *Ibid.*, 1760, p. 190.
[53] *Ibid.*, 1759, p. 59.
[54] *Ibid.*, 1772, p. 150.

On one occasion Hawley, who was suing for the return of a deed alleged to be held by one John Stewart of Colrain, received a tart and somewhat sarcastic letter from the defendant. Stewart wrote:

> Sr I read yours of Octr 6 wherein you inform of your information Thus & So—yr Letter Sr wears a very Threatening aspect. . . . Sr my character is So well known & my Innocence So Demonstrable in this matter That I neither was nor am afraid of all The consequents which might attend upon nor consequences which might follow a Prosecution in the affair—what Evidence my Father Thomson might be able to produce of my confession in the case I am not able To Say But this I have heard that in London Straw men are ready at a call—whether there be any such in Colrain I cant Tell—Yet Sure I am There are But few in it who really understand and fear an Oath & many who will Swear to their Imaginations—you have advised me 'to Deliver up the Deed peaceably' etc. Sr The Deed was Delivered up very peaceably many years agone & I never had it in my custody from That Day to this—I would be Glad that you now would advise my father Thomson to deliver up the fifty Pounds O.T. with the Interest of it for 11 years past which he is Like to and will (I'm afraid) Defraud me out of which yet remains unpaid. . . . Sr I am grieved that your place & Character exposes you often times to engage for Clients in Such causes as I am Satisfied you are Sorry for afterwards—I had conceived Such an opinion of you especially upon Seeing your public appearance in the case of the immortal (deservedly) & now Glorified Mr. Edwards as made one wish you might be Influenced & Determined by heaven to quit the Barr and resume the Pulpit—Hond Sr if you would be advised by me a poor illiterate mechanic To Leave The Law To The Lawyers (few of whom enter into The Kingdom of Heaven here or hereafter) & come over upon The Lord Side my Heart would rejoice ever more and The church of christ I hope would rejoice with me. . . .[55]

Some causes were obviously actions of tort. For instance, Phinehas Hannum of Belchertown in 1772 was alleged to have pulled down a fence between his property

---

[55] John Stewart to Hawley, Nov. 18, 1761. Among the Bancroft Papers, in a bundle catalogued as "Sermons Etc., of Joseph Hawley."

and that of his neighbor, Caleb Clarke. As a result Phinehas' cattle wandered into Caleb's corn and wheat, destroying much of it. Caleb sued successfully for £50 damages.[56] At another time Hawley acted for one Abraham Gibbs against Elisha Higgins who was defended by Worthington. In this case Elisha had beaten Abraham with a club and the latter claimed £20 as damages. When the court awarded Gibbs only £2/6/2 an appeal was carried to the higher court.[57] To this same category belonged suits like one by Noah and Rebecca Goodman against Benjamin Peirce. The plaintiffs, according to the formal and fictitious allegations in such actions, had lost a cow and yoke of oxen which were found by Peirce and although he knew that the cattle belonged to the Goodmans he never returned them. Hawley matched his talents against Worthington's in this action of trover and secured damages with costs for his clients, the owners of the wayward stock.[58]

Some comic relief is to be found in a few of Hawley's cases. Thomas Williams, a doctor, sued Timothy Childs to collect for drugs and medicines which he had administered to the defendant. Although Childs pleaded that "the Elixir Cortex and Bolus in the Plaintiff's account did him more hurt than Good," he lost his case.[59] A similar case was that of Benjamin Leonard vs. Timothy Cooper. Leonard's wife had fractured and injured her leg and Cooper, who professed to be a surgeon and bone-setter, was called in to practice his art. He promised to do a good job, but after binding the leg in splints and pouring rum over it for seven days, the patient was worse rather than better. Although she eventually recovered, her husband was long tormented by fears for her life. As a result he

[56] Common Pleas, 1772, p. 148. For discussion of the legal basis of an action of this sort see R. B. Morris, *Studies in the History of American Law*, pp. 208-25.
[57] *Ibid.*, 1763, p. 134.
[58] *Ibid.*, 1767, p. 117.
[59] *Ibid.*, 1763, p. 179.

## ATTORNEY AND BARRISTER 59

sued Cooper for damages of £40. The suit was futile, however, and the unfortunate Leonard found himself forced to pay costs of court.[60]

There is one instance of Hawley, along with Worthington, defending a client in a slander suit. John Morison, a minister of Colrain, had always possessed a good reputation but he had been called publicly a liar and a robber by one Charles Stewart and accused of preaching lies instead of Gospel truths. As a result the man of God had lost his reputation and his people were leaving his church. Stewart, although well defended, could not muster enough strength to win his case and he was ordered to pay Morison damages of £9.[61]

Suits were occasionally settled by resorting to arbitration. Such a solution was not restricted to any particular type of suit and while not generally used, it appears frequently enough to attract attention. For instance, in 1765, several millowners in Northampton sued one Samuel Kingsley for damages because he had built a dam on the Mill river below the plaintiffs' mills and had raised the water to a level which seriously hampered their operation. Hawley who defended Kingsley secured the submission of the dispute to arbitration, and eventually it was settled out of court.[62] Of an entirely different nature was the suit of Oliver Partridge and Obadiah Dickinson against Eleazer Burt. The three had formed a partnership to provision a Connecticut regiment stationed at Number Four (Charlestown, N. H.). Burt had been entrusted with the selling of the goods but had never given an accounting to his partners and the latter were seeking a settlement. Through Hawley, the case was settled by arbitration.[63]

The cases described were before the Court of Common Pleas or the Superior Court of Judicature, but they were

[60] *Ibid.*, 1766, p. 242.
[61] *Ibid.*, 1767, p. 182.
[62] *Ibid.*, 1765, p. 172.
[63] *Ibid.*, 1765, p. 113.

only part of his practice, although perhaps the most important from the purely legal point of view. Yet, as we have said, Hawley was a justice of the peace and this position entailed a great many legal and semi-judicial duties.

In the first place, he prepared the various legal documents which preceded or accompanied any action. Besides these he drew up literally hundreds of deeds for the conveyance of real estate.[64] He also issued warrants for the arrest of those involved in petty crimes or misdemeanors. In 1759, for example, one Samuel Scammon assisted by James Scammon deserted from the military company of Lieutenant Ebenezer Bardwell and the lieutenant sought a warrent for the arrest of James; Hawley issued this warrant.[65] At another time he issued a warrant to the constable on the petition of one Abiah Smith of Belchertown for the apprehension of her undoer, Moses Howe. Hawley issued the warrant and Moses was taken into custody, although his incarceration in Northampton was delayed by the impossibility of crossing the ice-filled Connecticut.[66] Again, Hawley took the deposition of one Samuel Phelps who under oath testified to his experiences in the army and sought his back pay. Hawley dispatched a memorial recording the facts to the authorities at Boston.[67]

His position brought him into close contact with the affairs of some of the nearby villages. The Hawley family had long been landowners in Pelham and perhaps for this reason Joseph Hawley was called upon in 1761 to issue warrants for two successive meetings of the town proprietors.[68] That town, as so many others, was troubled by a longstanding dispute over the common lands and roads. When the affair came to a head in 1767, the pro-

[64] Only a cursory examination of the miscellaneous papers of the Northampton families bears this fact out. See, for example, the Seth Pomeroy Papers or the Wells Papers.
[65] Hawley Papers, I.
[66] *Ibid.*, II.
[67] Mass. Archives, LXXIX, 20.
[68] C. O. Parmenter, *History of Pelham*, pp. 55, 59.

## ATTORNEY AND BARRISTER

prietors, unable to settle the matter by themselves, voted "that Joseph Hawley Esq. shall be consulted to see how we shall conduct ourselves in Selling the Roads and other Common Lands."[69] Hawley, as we shall see, had already distinguished himself by settling a similar dispute at Northampton and was a wise choice. But the problem was not solved at the first meeting and a few weeks later the proprietors met again and, still perplexed, voted "to bring Joseph Hawley Esq. out to our next meeting to counsel with him about our affairs in our present Difficulty."[70] Pelham was not the only town which called on Hawley. In the eastern part of the county the town of Ware had been settled by Scotch-Irish and English. These groups were always wrangling and after a time the quarrel was intensified by a division within the church, the Scotch-Irish supporting the minister against the English element. This dispute was at its height in 1752 when, in an attempt to force action upon the unwilling town officers, seven freeholders applied to Hawley as a justice of the peace for a warrant to hold a town meeting.[71] Whether Hawley issued the warrant or whether the meeting was ever held cannot be ascertained.

One duty of a justice of the peace was to sit on minor cases and where possible to mete out justice. The case of Porter vs. Phelps is an example. Porter had been sued by Phelps for some minor damages, and Hawley after hearing the evidence ordered the payment to the latter of damages of one penny and costs of £1/1/3. This was appealed to the next higher court where a jury reversed Hawley's settlement.[72] Many neighborhood quarrels and brawls must have come before him, but the records have long since disappeared.

[69] *Ibid.*, p. 61.
[70] *Ibid.*, p. 62.
[71] A. Chase, *History of Ware*, p. 74. According to Massachusetts law, if the selectmen of the town refused to call a town-meeting, the citizens might secure a warrant for a meeting from a justice of the peace.
[72] Common Pleas, 1750, p. 88.

At the Court of General Sessions Hawley was involved in the government of the county. At different times he was on committees for the repair of the courthouse at Northampton and for the disposal of materials used in these repairs.[73] His activity in securing a site for the new courthouse in 1767 has already been noticed. The laying out of new roads, a most important part of county government, also fell to him or to committees of which he was a member.[74] Very early in his service at this court he was on a committee to settle the accounts of the county treasurers.[75] It was all routine work but highly necessary.

The Court of General Sessions was in part a criminal court and the cases in which Hawley was engaged were often redolent of a rustic society. They concerned generally the support of illegitimate children and were extremely numerous. Of more interest are other prosecutions. At Hawley's instance, Ebenezer Pomeroy, an innholder of Hadley, was brought into court for allowing "sundry couples of young people belonging to Northampton . . . to sing dance and revel in sd house and then to continue this singing dancing and revelling one whole night." It cost Ebenezer ten shillings and costs of court.[76] In 1761 Josiah Lyman of Belchertown was charged with forcibly entering a pew in a house of worship and interrupting the services. Hawley defended him and secured a quashing of the charge.[77] At another time Hawley acted for the proprietors of Falltown (Bernardston) against the suit of the Crown for failing to keep the highway in repair. By refusing to contend against the Crown, the proprietors escaped with paying the costs of court.[78] In 1763 Hawley was "attorney for our Lord the King," apparently the only time he held that honor, in a prosecution against one Jonathan Kil-

[73] General Sessions, 1757, p. 250; 1760, p. 168.
[74] *Ibid.*, 1753, p. 207.
[75] *Ibid.*, 1751, p. 119.
[76] *Ibid.*, 1759, p. 96.
[77] *Ibid.*, 1761, p. 270.
[78] *Ibid.*, 1759, p. 93.

## ATTORNEY AND BARRISTER

bourn for killing deer at Monson.[79] Somehow one is surprised to find Hawley practicing before the court of which he was a justice, but as the years went by he ceased to act in this court except on its bench.

Towards the end of his years at the bar, in 1772, he formed a partnership with Joseph Clarke, his adopted son, for the collection of debts with or without actions at law. Part of the agreement for the partnership throws light on the methods of the time, for it is stated that according to custom the partners should advance all fees and charges in these suits until final judgment should be received. Compensation for services and disbursements would then be secured by taking the whole sum of the bill of costs awarded by the court.[80] It is more than likely that this partnership was formed in order to give the younger man a start in the profession; certainly by 1772 Hawley was so well established and so occupied with public life that extra practice could not have interested him.

One case in which Hawley was concerned was of great importance in its results, for it gave him province-wide publicity and pointed the way to his leadership in the anti-government party. It was the celebrated "Berkshire Affair." Hawley's own account of the trial gives an insight into his knowledge of law and his method of pleading, as well as all the details of what became a *cause célèbre*.

The affair grew out of the Stamp Act and the resistance to its enforcement. During the summer and fall of 1765 successive riots and organized opposition had put an end to all distribution or sale of the stamps. But as stamps were required on all legal documents, the normal channels of justice were clogged. In the late fall at the village of Lanesborough in Berkshire County a complicated situation existed. Stamps were unobtainable, and as a result, legal action was paralyzed. This situation was particularly hard

[79] *Ibid.*, 1763, p. 160.
[80] Hawley Papers, II.

on all who were imprisoned for debt, since they found it impossible to secure the customary bond which would have allowed them the freedom of the jail-yard.[81] The situation was discussed among the citizens of the region until at a house raising on the sixth of November, a group agreed not to permit any more arrests for debt until the king's writ could be secured, guaranteeing the rights of debtors. The same night a deputy sheriff named Morse visited the village tavern and there happening upon one John Franklin against whom he had an execution, arrested him and also one Peter Curtis for whom he had another writ. Immediately the cry arose that the sheriffs were come and a general mêlée followed; yet in spite of the free use of staves and stones no one was seriously injured. Morse and his party soon deemed it prudent to withdraw to Pittsfield.[82] This was only the beginning.

In the spring the Grand Jury for Berkshire County indicted ten of those involved in the fracas of the preceding November and presented them for trial at the April sitting of the Court of General Sessions of the Peace at Great Barrington. Of these ten only Seth Warren, the ringleader, pleaded not guilty to the charge of riot and unlawful assembly. Nevertheless the jury found him guilty and sentenced him to pay a fine of £3.[83] So far the case had seemed only of minor importance; in fact, no different from many others which came before the provincial courts from time to time.

Hawley, who was Warren's attorney, advised him to appeal to the Superior Court, on the grounds that, first, the writ of execution for the arrest of Franklin was not stamped and therefore gave the officer no authority to make any arrest; second, that as the company was peaceably assembled together, the action of Warren and the others

[81] The limits of the jail-yard might be construed, and often were, so as to give the prisoner the limits of the entire town.
[82] Boston *Evening Post*, Jan. 5, 1767.
[83] *Ibid.*, Jan. 5, 1767.

was not the result of plotting and the affray was not riot but trespass; and third, that considering conditions within the province, it was entirely possible that in the end the attorney-general would decide to enter a *nolle prosequi*. While Hawley admitted afterward that these reasons for appeal might have been faulty, his advice was followed and Warren's appeal found its way to the docket of the Superior Court sitting at Springfield in September, 1766.[84]

There, before Chief Justice Hutchinson, Judge Cushing and Judge Oliver, the Berkshire yeoman and his attorney fought their case.[85] The old evidence was introduced and reviewed carefully. Hawley insisted that the affair had been trespass not riot. He also pointed out that at the time of the affair the courts were closed, that the king's writs were not obtainable, and that conditions were so extraordinary that what might be considered criminal in ordinary times, in this instance might well be regarded in a different light. Peter Oliver, who prosecuted for the king, emphasized the previous agreement between Warren and his fellows as proof that the riot and assault were committed as a result of a so-called conspiracy. The chief justice in his charge to the jury insisted that in the opinion of the court, riot had occurred and that Warren should be found guilty.[86]

The jury was charged in the late afternoon, and the court then adjourned until morning for the verdict and the sentence. During the night Hawley pondered over the case and suddenly came to the conclusion that if, as the justices had alleged, the affair was the result of "confederacy and agreement," then his client was guilty of much more than riot, in fact, guilty of high treason. He thus came to feel that if this new view were presented, he could secure either a *nolle prosequi* or a dismissal and a new charge against Seth Warren. Incidentally, a jury would not be

[84] *Ibid.*, July 6, 1767.
[85] *Ibid.*, July 6, 1767.
[86] *Ibid.*, July 13, 1767.

likely to bring in a conviction on a charge of treason. Therefore the next morning when the jury came in, Hawley cited Hawkin's *Pleas of the Crown* to the chief justice to show that according to the evidence presented, his client had been guilty of treason.[87] Hutchinson agreed that it was probably "sound doctrine and clear law" but nevertheless Warren was found guilty and sentenced to pay a fine of £3 and costs.[88]

Hawley defended his position in a series of letters to the Boston *Evening Post* which controverted a similar series by "Philanthrop." In the letter published on July 13, 1767 his argument is brilliantly stated. The question there examined is whether Warren "was guilty of any crime at all cognizable at law." Maintaining that circumstances alter cases, he proceeded to examine the state of the province at the time of the "Berkshire Affair." His discovery was startling; the people of Massachusetts Bay were outlawed in the sense that they were deprived of the benefit of the law without crime or offense of their own, because the courts did not exercise their jurisdiction nor did the king's writ run. Lord Coke was quoted to substantiate this hypothesis of unjust outlawry. Continuing, Hawley argued: "Is it not most plain that at the very instant the positive laws of the society (that is, those laws which are grounded on the civil compact) cease or are suspended, the laws of nature must emerge and take place...." In his opinion, on that fateful November night a state of nature existed and Warren with his fellows resisted only the exercise of arbitrary and unjust force; all should then have been acquitted. In conclusion he maintained: "Of that opinion I believe all those will be, who *have the principles of the English constitution interwoven with the constitution of their mind:* Of that opinion I believe *Lord Holt* would have been, if the trial had been before *him*; and I believe

[87] *Ibid.*
[88] Hawley Papers, I. Extract from minute book of Superior Court for counties of Hampshire and Berkshire, Sept. 1766.

he would have so enlightened the jury in the case, that they would with great clearness have acquitted the said Warren."[89]

Hawley's letters in the Boston *Evening Post* left little doubt as to his opinion of Chief Justice Hutchinson and his associates in the trial. His comments on them were probably highly injudicious, especially at a time of general unrest, but they were not as the Superior Court maintained, "injurious and scandalous Reflections." While the sensation caused by these letters was still fresh Hutchinson wrote to John Cushing: "What shall we do with Hawley?" I can freely forgive him but how shall we save the honour of the court? Brother Lynde says it will never do to suffer him to plead before us without some submission. I am not sure that he will be of the same mind when we come to Springfield."[90] But when they came to Springfield the minds of the judges were made up; they considered the matter of the articles and after a little reflection ordered that Hawley's name "be struck out of the Rolls of the Barristers and Attorneys of this Court, & that he do not hereafter appear or act as a Barrister or Attorney of this Court."[91] It was the court's turn to be injudicious.

The victim of this disbarment was not at all subdued by the proceedings; on the contrary he rose to new attacks upon the court. He publicly declared that he could see no wrong in telling the details of a cause tried in the king's court nor in passing observations on the prosecution "for if every man's mouth is to be sealed up, and nothing may be said or wrote relative thereto, and the trial had almost as good be had only in the cool light of the lawless court and in the secrecy and darkness of a Romish inquisition."[92] Hawley agreed that if the court were in-

[89] Boston *Evening Post*, July 13, 1767.
[90] *Mass. Hist. Soc. Pro.*, Series III, Vol. IV, p. 524.
[91] Superior Court, 1767, p. 46.
[92] Boston *Evening Post*. Jan. 18, 1768. A draft of this in the author's handwriting is to be found in the Hawley Papers, I.

fallible, criticism of its conduct would be blasphemy, but he knew of only "one tribunal absolutely infallible and that not the said court." Furthermore he had never imagined that any attorney upon being admitted to the bar relinquished any of the "common rights and liberties of his fellow subjects," and one in particular—freedom of speech. Then with an appeal for sympathy, he wrote: "But admitting, after all, that any of my remarks were rather free, and beyond what consumate prudence would have dictated: *sed quere* whether the court would not have shown as much true magnanimity, and as effectually preserved their honor, and dignity, by a total disregard and neglect of them, as by their late measure of depriving, without any trial before indifferent Judges, a poor country Attorney, of his practice, which is truly his freehold. . . ."[93]

Disbarment however, was only temporary. At the next sitting of the Superior Court at Springfield, John Worthington secured Hawley's restoration to his old standing.[94] Meanwhile, as we shall see, Hawley had had his revenge. Never again did he become involved in any case which attracted such general attention. Instead, he continued his simple practice until once more the king's courts were closed and the king's writ did not run; then he put aside his barrister's gown forever.

[93] Ibid., Jan. 18, 1768.
[94] Bliss, *op. cit.*, p. 39.

CHAPTER V

A "RIVER GOD"

Eighteenth-century Massachusetts society despite its apparent simplicity was complex. Whether a member of a particular profession, merchant or farmer, every man busied himself with a variety of interests whose sum total made existence possible. Except in the largest towns most men carried on some farming, trading, or both, whatever their regular occupations. If a man had a little extra money he was apt to speculate in land; and the situation being what it was, he and most of his companions had military experience. Between times they were the heads of households and in them knew the joys and sorrows of private and family life. So it was with Hawley.

During these years Joseph Hawley found that family and personal matters demanded as much thought and attention as did the larger affairs of state and profession. His public career might cast the greater shadow but his private life was no less real or important. For a few years after his return from Louisbourg he and his brother were in a partnership for "carrying on the trades in goods and silver" and in 1747, Seth Dwight, a fellow townsman, was added to form a company for trafficking in deerskins. These skins were bought in the surrounding countryside, sometimes even as far away as Albany, dressed in Northampton, and then sold by agents in Massachusetts and the neighboring provinces.[1] The following letter from Hawley to his brother gives an insight into this business:

You desire in yours that I would let You known how Timo Dwight disposed of leather—he returned last week on Wednesday and gives but a dull account, he went a little round about to Rhode Island, and was not able (as

[1] Trumbull, *op. cit.*, II, 547.

he Says) to Market any leather, heard to people's talk that the Country was glutted with leather, got discouraged, left 75 lb. of leather at Rhode Island with one Bonnet, brought about 20 lb. home with him, having Sold but 4 skins. We have Sent out Doct[r] King from Hatfield with a good pack. Josiah Searl is to Set out this day with about 60 lb. to market it if can, Then to go to Rhode Island, take what Dwight left there and market that.[2]

Eventually the pressure of other affairs and the coming of the last French and Indian War caused the enterprise to be abandoned.

Even during their partnership Elisha Hawley was absent much of the time as a soldier on the frontier. He had been in the service as early as 1746, and in that year was among those whom Northampton rewarded by exemption from the payment of a poll tax.[3] Generally he was stationed at Fort Massachusetts, the most important post in a string of forts which early in King George's War had been built through the western hills of Massachusetts and what is now southern Vermont. Fort Massachusetts was always a dangerous outpost and in 1746 had been captured by a force of French and Indians. At first Elisha was only a sergeant, but in March of 1747 he received a lieutenant's commission from his uncle, Colonel John Stoddard, and was placed in command of the fort.[4]

Throughout this and later periods of service Elisha Hawley was in constant receipt of letters of advice from Joseph who urged him to "observe as you value your Soul, as you value your honor and Credit in the world and particularly your Credit and influence with and on the garrison viz that your conversation be Serious, Savoury, manly and genteel, as becomes a Christian and a man of honour, and Not unsavoury, Smutty or profane."[5] Again Joseph reminded him to give "intelligence and the State

[2] Hawley to Elisha, Feb. 16, 1747-8. Hawley Papers, I, 6.
[3] Trumbull, *op. cit.*, II, 157.
[4] *Ibid.*, II, 154.
[5] Hawley to Elisha, Dec. 25, 1747. Hawley Papers, I.

and provision of the Garrison with respect to Eatables and warlike Stores to those whose business is to provide that So the blame may never be devolved on you if mischief Should happen through defect of that. Take heed you be not surprized through carelessness which is a very ignoble cause of Mischief."[6] In one of the many skirmishes about the fort, Elisha received a charge of buckshot in the calf of his leg and news of this mishap somewhat excited his family. In a letter accompanying provisions and remedies from home, Joseph wrote to the soldier brother, "Mother is pretty much concerned about you, but not so much as I feared she would have been . . . . [She] has given me Some Sarve to Send you which She thinks best to put above your wound to prevent the humours from falling into the wound as She imagines you will be inclined to Stir a pretty deal."[7] But peace between Great Britain and France was signed October 18, 1748, and thereafter there was less occasion to "Stir a pretty deal" although sporadic Indian raids continued for another year.

At intervals during the war Elisha had been with his brother and widowed mother at the old home in Pudding Lane. Although Rebekah's boys had grown to man's estate, they were far from independent of their domineering mother. Once when she discovered that Elisha was a too frequent vistor at the home of a girl socially the inferior of the Hawleys, she reasoned and pled with him and when he persisted, followed him one night to the girl's home, called him out, and then resolutely took him home. But in the long run all her vigilance and supervision were to no purpose. Elisha became involved in an affair with a village girl, one Martha Root. There were twins and a pretty scandal. It became a public affair when the Northampton church excommunicated Elisha and the civil power took up the case. Elisha, again on the frontier and beyond the range of the clattering tongues, allowed Joseph to manage his case.

[6] *Ibid.*, Feb. 16, 1747-8. Hawley Papers, I, 6.
[7] *Ibid.*, Aug. 12, 1748. Hawley Papers, I, 11.

The Roots, possibly because they were dealing with one of the town's leading families, were not easily appeased, and Joseph was forced to write his brother that his management of the affair was not too successful. When he attempted to secure a settlement the Roots demanded £150, but as this seemed too great a sum, a continuance was secured from the court. But, he wrote, "I hope before next Session I Shall accomodate the affair upon easier Terms than they Seem at present to insist upon, if not I Should think it best to abide the order of the Court but I hope to have the opportunity to inform you further of the affair ere long."[8] In the end to quiet the whole matter, Elisha paid Martha £155 and secured her release from all further claims upon him.[9]

While the Roots were now silenced, the attitude of the church was unrelenting, and Joseph was forced to try to secure a settlement which would bring Elisha back into the fold. The stand taken by the church seemed extreme to him, and late in the year he wrote to his brother, "were I in the case I Should have no regard at all to anything they pretended to do authoritatively in the particular of matrimony, nor would I attempt to labour to prove anything against her Since the burden of proof, beyond all dispute lies wholly on either the woman or the Church as they are respectively Considered as acting. ... All therefore I at present would do (let the Church take what Course they would) Should be to offer them a proper Confession, and rest the Matter as to Matrimony. I would Do what I knew was right in Conscience and before God."[10]

Ultimately a council of ministers sat at Northampton to settle the "grievances between the Church and Lt. Hawley." Joseph appeared before the council and argued his brother's case, basing it, without too much truth, on

[8] *Ibid.*, Feb. 16, 1747/8. Hawley Papers, I, 6.
[9] Hawley Papers, I, 7.
[10] Hawley to Elisha, Dec. 23, 1748. Hawley Papers, I, 12.

Martha Root's being a woman of the town.[11] Whether influenced by Hawley's excited pleading, the family's high position in Northampton, or by the remembrance of the scriptural command about casting the first stone, the council was unable to see its way clear to require that Elisha should marry Martha Root. Instead it practically decided in his favor, voting: "We . . . . apprehend It must be left to the Determination of his own Conscience, and upon the whole we recommend it to the first church of Northampton to receive Mr. Hawley (upon his making a penitent confession of the Sin of fornication) to their Christian charity and fellowship again."[12] So it was done and Elisha went his way, Martha hers. But soon Elisha, although still spending much of his time on the frontier, began to think of settling down. He had had his fling and now was courting Elizabeth Pomeroy, the niece of Seth Pomeroy and the daughter of respected and well-known citizens of the town, Ebenezer and Elizabeth Pomeroy. In the spring of 1751 he bought a homestead and houselot of more than six acres and here a few months later he brought his bride.[13]

Joseph also was contemplating matrimony and much to his mother's disgust was giving his attentions to Mercy Lyman, a daughter of the prominent citizen, Joseph Lyman. Madame Hawley could find no fault with Mercy's social standing, but took refuge in the comment that she had a face like a toasting-iron, although others found Mercy a beautiful girl and considered her a beauty even at seventy.[14]

[11] Hawley later asked Martha for her forgiveness because of the exaggerated statements he had made on this occasion. Letter of Hawley to Martha Root, Aug. 8, 1750. Hawley Papers, I, 10.

[12] Hawley Papers, I, 9.

[13] The deed to Elisha's homestead is among the Hawley Papers. His marriage is recorded in the Northampton Town Records, Births, Marriages, Deaths, I, 116.

[14] The *Hampshire Gazette* (Northampton) for June 15, 1852 cites this story in a brief memoir of Rebekah Hawley by Sylvester Judd.

Mercy was living or visiting at Brookfield much of the time and while distance might lend enchantment, it did not make for a very speedy courtship. Possibly for this reason the romance dragged along, although Joseph visited Mercy frequently and apparently was anxious to bring matters to a head. He wrote Elisha early in the spring of 1750: "As to my Matrimonials I cant say a great deal abt it in this Epistle. I have visited M—y several times the winter past, and have not a month since been to Brookfield . . . what another visit may determine I cant say—but I design if Providence permit, to make another visit Shortly as Consists with good Judgement and policy."[15] Somehow, in spite of frequent visits and all due attention to good policy, another year found Joseph still single, still visiting at Brookfield, and still hopefully writing, although with a touch of cynicism now: "If I don't mistake the matter gets along as fast the other side as it does on mine. . . . But such affairs are very subject to mutation."[16] At last, late in 1752, they were married and Mercy came to the Hawley homestead on Pudding Lane to commence life with a singularly devoted husband.

As long as Madame Hawley lived she never wholly accepted Mercy and lived much by herself in rooms apart from her son and daughter-in-law. The year after their marriage she built an addition to the house for a cheese room and buttery and devoted more of her time than ever to cheese making.[17] Morning and evening she joined the family at prayers, but if any unusual noise arose in the barnyard, she would hitch her chair quietly to the window until she could see what the commotion was about.[18] The new-fangled custom of tea-drinking never met with her approval; it was a waste of good money and besides Joseph's wife liked it. When Madame Hawley was away

[15] Hawley to Elisha. March 11, 1750. Hawley Papers, I.
[16] *Ibid.*, June 17, 1751. Hawley Papers, I.
[17] Trumbull, *op. cit.*, II, 82.
[18] Judd Manuscript, I, 193.

from the house Mercy and her friends would hastily get out the tea things, but even then some one had to stand guard at the window to give the alarm if the feared mother-in-law should appear in sight. Gradually the years began to tell on Rebekah; the allotted three score years and ten were extended to four score until on a June day in 1766, she was laid to rest in the old burying ground.[19]

Joseph Hawley can scarcely be regarded as a land speculator, perhaps because throughout life he had a striking disregard for the accumulation of wealth. He inherited considerable land, both in Northampton and Pelham; gradually he purchased small parcels of pasture and tillage in Northampton. But except for one very small venture, he apparently never speculated. In 1752, when what is now Williamstown was being settled, both Joseph and Elisha purchased lots in the new town. These lots contained only about eleven acres and cost £6/13/4. Joseph sold his lot eleven years later and thereafter did not trouble about similar purchases.[20]

Meanwhile there was war again. The peace of Aix-la-Chapelle was little more than a truce, a breathing space for both contestants in their struggle for a continent. Throughout the period the most important forts on the Massachusetts frontier were garrisoned and Elisha Hawley, now a captain, was periodically in command in the post at the foot of Mt. Greylock, Fort Massachusetts. In 1754, two years before war was formally declared between Great Britain and France, hostilities began along the colonial frontiers. As Colonel Israel Williams, a cousin of the Hawleys, wrote: "it is now open war and a very dark distressing scene opens; a merciless miscreant enemy invading us in every quarter, pushed on by our inveterate foe."[21] In this new war Joseph Hawley was to play a more active part than in the last when, except for his chaplaincy

[19] *Ibid.*, I, 193.
[20] A. L. Perry, *Origins in Williamstown*, p. 383.
[21] Trumbull, *op. cit.*, II, 245.

in the Louisbourg expedition and his participation in several armed forays to "Scoure the frontier," he had devoted his energies to the calls of civilian life. Although at the end of the last war he had been only a corporal, he was to be a major in this, and was to be known as Major Hawley during the rest of his life.[22]

The war actually began far from Massachusetts when George Washington, sent by Governor Dinwiddie of Virginia into western Pennsylvania, clashed with a French force at Great Meadows in May, 1754. Although in New England the war was not felt until late summer, the troops in Hampshire County were under arms during August, and Joseph Hawley was in regular correspondence with Colonel Israel Williams about the organization of the militia. In Hawley's opinion it was "much best to make the least alteration possible"in the officers of the Hampshire regiment, and his advice to a large extent was accepted.[23] Early in September Indians were reported near Southampton, and the juggling of officers' commissions gave place to an active mobilization of the county's forces. On September 8, Colonel Williams ordered Major Hawley to enlist ten men for service at Southampton, and this order was complied with the next morning, even if the men did set out insufficiently supplied with powder and flints.[24] Southampton, at this and for some time before, had been on edge for fear of an Indian attack; in fact one Sunday during divine worship, "the assembly broke up in sermon time by a gun shot at a bare."[25] For many months after this incident Southampton was garrisoned but the inhabitants continued to be in a highly nervous state.

[22] On the muster roll of Colonel Joseph Dwight's company for 1748, Hawley is listed as a corporal. Mass. Archives, XCII, 134.
[23] Hawley to Israel Williams, Aug. 16, 1754. Israel William Papers, 72. Mass. Hist. Soc.
[24] *Ibid.*, Sept. 9, 1754. I. Williams Papers, 86.
[25] From an entry in the minister's diary, quoted in Trumbull, *op. cit.*, II, 247.

Major Hawley after one of many alarums at Southampton reported at length to Israel Williams:

Yesterday about 3 o'clock P.M. an enemy was at Southampton about a mile from Mr. Judd's. Two men and some lads were picking corn, and one man carting corn. Two soldiers were on guard, one at the bars of the field and the other at the opposite of the field. The carter was gone with a load of corn, and returning. Higgins (the guard) at the bars supposed he heard some one stir in the brush (which were very thick) near him. He turned and faced the place where he heard the noise, upon which a gun was discharged, which shot the left thigh of his trousers through on the crotch side, with a ball and three swan shot, but missed his flesh. . . . I was inclined to think the fellow had shot his own breeches with a view to make noise, but the people who went out are satisfied the fellow was shot by an enemy. The people in the field say he came to them as soon after they heard the gun as was possible for a man to come, and his gun was then loaded with two balls; he appeared in the utmost consternation. His brother soldiers proposed to go to the spot but he said "for Lord's sake don't go there." The soldiers and laborers all immediately fled from the field at the opposite part to the nearest house that way. The fellow appears innocent and uniform in his account. No person had been where the tracks were discovered. The most considerate at Southampton and diverse of those who before were infidels reporting the enemy's being with them are satisfied that the enemy was in fact there. . . . If the enemy are gone, sending men this day will be of no service. If they are not made off they will be there on the morrow. Therefore propose not to send any men out today it being the Sabbath without your positive order—propose to send out a sutiable number tomorrow early to Southampton to secure those parts and a part west where they may be most likely to come thwart the Indians or their tracks if they have or are returning.[26]

Even in time of stress and danger the provincials found it difficult to coöperate or to work unitedly in the defense of the frontier. Major Hawley who considered that his ideas for the defense of the regions west of the Con-

[26] Hawley to Israel Williams, Sept. 22, 1754. I. Williams Papers, 72.

necticut were as good as anyone else's found himself, or at least thought he did, ignored by the other officers of the county. Colonel Israel Williams and Major Ephraim Williams devised schemes without consulting Hawley and placed them before the governor; Colonel Oliver Partridge likewise drew up plans which he submitted for consideration. But Hawley insisted that the best results could be obtained only if all together worked out a general scheme which could be supported in the legislature by the representatives from the county. It was particularly embarrassing for Hawley, a member of the legislature, to hear the various plans for the first time while sitting in the House. Of all this Hawley wrote in great exasperation to Israel Williams, concluding his argument for concerted leadership with the obvious point that if plans were to meet with the legislature's approval, they must have the support of the members from Hampshire. As he said, "Altho, I am a person of but Small Consideration Yet If Providence Should so order It that I Should be in the house when these matters Should be Considered, If there appears Sinister designs interwoven in the plans It will be no difficult matter to prevent their taking. I dont think that in my private Capacity I am of much importance as to Such matters but as a member of the house, It is possible I may be, for I have always Spoke my mind in the house and sometimes have been heard. And If providence Should give me opportunity probably I shall be as free as usual respecting affairs this way especially."[27]

Hampshire County at this time was very much under the control of the Williams family, and particularly of Israel Williams of Hatfield. After the death of Colonel John Stoddard in 1748, Israel Williams became commander of the military forces in the county. Autocratic and domineering, wealthy, supported by his numerous cousins, and enjoying favor with the successive governors of the province, his position in the county seemed impreg-

[27] *Ibid.*, Oct. 3, 1754. I. Williams Papers, 88.

nable. But he was soon to discover that one cousin, Joseph Hawley, would not be his unquestioning supporter. The little difference in 1754 was only a warning of what was to be a lifelong disagreement.

The war kept on its uncertain course and gradually the Hampshire leaders learned to work together. As 1754 drew to a close Hawley was busy with a committee of fellow officers, supervising the expenditure of funds for the building and repairing of the forts on the western frontier.[28] When the new year opened, Governor Shirley with his customary vigor began preparations for a campaign against Crown Point, one of the important French posts on Lake Champlain; as part of these preparations a regiment of 500 men was to be raised in Hampshire County. The work of recruiting started in March. Hawley, as the Northampton representative in the legislature received all instructions and necessary papers from Governor Shirley, and with Israel and Ephraim Williams and Oliver Partridge raised and organized the force.[29] On April 9, he wrote to his colleagues urging them to hasten enlistments while popular enthusiasm was still high and also recommending that Seth Pomeroy should be lieutenant-colonel of the regiment.[30] By mid-June the regiment was ready to set out for Albany; Seth Pomeroy was second in command and Elisha Hawley was captain of one of the companies.[31]

Although much of the war seemed far away at Lake George and Lake Champlain, there were alarums again at Southampton that summer and Major Hawley drew up plans for its defense. As he wrote to Israel Williams: "I apprehend It reasonable on the whole That if they will either Picquet the houses or Surround them with a high

[28] Trumbull, *op. cit.*, II, 249.
[29] Shirley to I. Williams, March 29, 1755. Quoted in Perry, *Origins in Williamstown*, p. 300. For a general discussion of this campaign see Osgood, *op. cit.*, IV, 362-67.
[30] Hawley to I. Williams, *et al.*, April 9, 1755. I. Williams Papers, 122.
[31] Trumbull, *op. cit.*, II, 252.

board fence which Shall be tight and erect flankers It will be reasonable that the Ten Soldiers proposed for them Should be distributed and assigned to three places viz To Mr. Judd's house four, Nathan Lyman's house three, and three to Jehahad Strong's house. That the Inhabitants work in three Companies and that the Soldiers keep the Sd three houses where I propose the Women and Children Should reside."[32] But Southampton, whatever its fate might be, was only a leaf in the storm.

Meanwhile the Hampshire regiment moved into the province of New York and by July, in company with other troops from Massachusetts, New York and Rhode Island it formed part of a great expedition under Sir William Johnson and Phinehas Lyman of Suffield which moved slowly up the Hudson above Albany. After nearly two months of slow, tedious marching this force of about three thousand men reached the lower end of Lake George. At the same time the French under Baron Dieskau with an army of French and Indians were marching south from Ticonderoga to defeat Johnson and, if possible, take the newly completed Fort Edward. English scouts discovered traces of this hostile force on the eighth of September and reported to Sir William Johnson that the French and their allies were close at hand but that they were apparently retreating. Elisha Hawley was writing to his brother at the moment that this report was brought in:

I suppose 'tis the fixed determination of the chief officers of the army, to proceed to Crown Point, as soon as we are joined by the recruits that we hear are raised, 'tis apprehended the consequences of our returning without going thro' with what was projected when we set out would be so fatal that I believe we shall be ordered to proceed altho' our Numbers should not be the Numbers that we are informed are at Crown Point. . . . While I am writing one of our Scouts who has just come in informs that the day before yesterday they discovered a little west of the drowned Land the tracks of a very large body of French and Indians,

---

[32] Hawley to I. Williams, July 11, 1755. I. Williams Papers, 151.

who were just gone. . . . I am this minute a going out in company with five hundred men to see if we can intercept 'em in their retreat, or find their canoes in the drowned Land, and therefore must conclude this letter.[33]

So Elisha and his fellow soldiers set out on what history knows as the "bloody morning scout" or the battle of Lake George. About three miles from their camp they ran into an ambush and in the deadly fighting which followed fell some of the flower of Hampshire County. Colonel Ephraim Williams, whose estate would eventually help to found a famous college, was "shot Dead in a moment & before he had Time to Fire his Gun." Elisha Hawley was mortally wounded.[34] He lingered for a fortnight but on September 24, Seth Pomeroy was forced to record in his journal: "At 7 of the clock at night Capt. Hawley died of the wound he received in the memorable battle Sept. 8."[35]

At Northampton they had been waiting anxiously for news of the wounded man, but when word finally brought the account of his death "the family was all in an uproar, confusion filled the house, and distraction every one in it."[36] On the older brother now fell all the care and responsibilities of the family. Life had to go on, of course, but Joseph used his position as town clerk to inscribe sorrowfully on the town records:

"*Sept. 24, 1755* Capt. Elisha Hawley of Northampton of the grievous wounds which he rec$^d$ in the Bloody Battle fought on the 8th of said September near Lake George formerly called Lake Sacrament—he died in the Camp near said Lake and there lies interred—

> The sweetest Form there Worms Consume
> His Brothers Breast a Living Tomb
> The dearest Image safe contain
> Till the same Features rise again
> —Hubbard

[33] Elisha to Joseph, Sept. 8, 1755. Hawley Papers, I.

[34] Seth Pomeroy to his wife. Quoted in Trumbull, *op. cit.*, II, 283.

[35] Journal of Seth Pomeroy. Reproduced completely in Trumbull, *op. cit.*, II, 260-280.

[36] From the fragment of a letter from Hawley in answer to a letter of condolence. In the Hawley Papers.

> O! my Brother Thou wast slain in thy High Places
> I am distressed for thee my Brother very pleasant
> hast thou been unto me
>
> —J. Hawley[37]

The "bloody morning scout," however harshly it fell on Hampshire County, was inconclusive, and the struggle went on, although between Great Britain and France war had yet to be declared officially. Hampshire County's enthusiasm for the war was dying and never again would it be at the pitch of the first years. Yet its men fought along the frontiers for several years longer. There were Acadians in the town now and the people had the rare treat of seeing Papists in the flesh; but that was only one more of the social effects of the war.[38] The war came closer again in the summer of 1756 when eight soldiers were killed in an ambush near Fort Massachusetts, and the French were rumoured to be in the western forests of the province. Major Hawley in great excitement wrote to Israel Williams: "Should It prove that there is an army there and Either one or both of the forts Should be taken, you S$^r$ never will be pardoned if you don't Send militia." But the Major himself found it inconvenient to go to the forts for two reasons, "the one that the Weather is so Extremely hot that I would Instantly Bring the disorder to which I am Incident in hot weather, the other is that It is a very pressing time in the business of my profession and Some other affairs which Claim my particular attention at this time."[39] So the Major begged off and shifted responsibility to his cousin. The situation still seemed most serious to him and he "never Saw so much reason for a most humble and circumspect behaviour and for Crying to God that he would take off my heart from Vanity . . . and turn it fully to himself and heaven and that he would

---

[37] Northampton Town Records, Births, Marriages, Deaths, I, 161.

[38] Hawley was a member of the committee which apportioned sixty-seven Acadians in Hampshire County in 1760. *Mass. Acts and Resolves*, XVI, 554.

[39] Hawley to I. Williams, July 13, 1756. I. Williams Papers, 226.

Spare and help his people (If we of this land may yet be Called So) who are brought very low."[40] Amid all the excitement Hawley's house was a headquarters for military men and for military councils, mixed up with impressment officers and men seeking to escape impressment, for the people were growing faint-hearted and war-weary, and soldiers were raised only with difficulty.[41]

So the months passed; sometimes the endless war seemed very near at hand, but often very far away. A disaster in August, 1757, awoke the people to realities and spread new fears through western Massachusetts. Fort William Henry at the lower end of Lake George was captured by a force of French and Indians on August 9, and following the surrender many of the garrison were massacred by liquor-crazed Indians. The loss of the fort laid New York and Massachusetts open to attack, but the seriousness of the danger inspired almost a mass rising of the people. In Hampshire County so many went to the relief of the fort that the county seemed almost evacuated, at least of all able-bodied men, for all the militia marched to the scene of the disaster.[42] Major Hawley had been ordered to start towards the fort even before its fall and although he had protested against setting out, apparently had obeyed orders.[43] While on the march he wrote to his wife from Sheffield: "We are proceeding as fast as we well can towards Ft. Edward." When the regiment reached Kinderhook, New York, it turned back and in less than a fortnight from the time of its setting out was back again at Northampton.[44]

From now on the war prospered for the English. Hampshire County supplied troops, carts and provisions when

[40] *Ibid.*, July 16, 1756. I. Williams Papers, 230.

[41] *Ibid.*, Sept. 15-16, 1756. I. Williams Papers, 258, 261.

[42] Gen. Pepperell to Capt. Christie. Quoted in Trumbull, *op. cit.*, II, 291.

[43] Hawley to Williams, Aug. 8, 1757. I. Williams Papers, 71, E34.

[44] Mass. Archives, XCIX, 1.

called upon, but with reluctance if the calls happened to interfere with seed-time or harvest. In 1760, when the American phase of the world conflict was nearly over, a last Indian raid occurred at Colrain in the northern part of Hawley's county. Most of the effective militia being in Canada, Hawley hastily raised a small force and set out for the scene of the attack. When it became apparent that pursuit of the Indians was futile, the men soon returned.[45] This incident was the last of the war for most of them and gradually the other Northampton men in the army drifted back into peace-time occupations. Finally with the end of the war in 1763, not a single Northampton name was on the active list of the province muster rolls.

Yet in spite of these recurring wars and rumors of wars, town life went on serenely and concerned itself with the homelier side of existence. At town meeting people were arguing about the removal of pigsties from the town lands, the reseating of the meeting house, and the building of horsesheds; measures for the prosecution of war were not worth noting in the town records. Besides, there was the perennial dispute with the town proprietors which never failed to arouse more bitter passions than the prospect of even hand-to-hand fighting with the subjects of His Most Christian Majesty and his redskin allies.

The intricacies of Massachusetts town organization lent themselves to disagreements and disputes which in a day without political parties had all the earmarks of strife within an oversized family. On the one hand was a political organism called the town, a relatively simple thing and democratic in theory if not in practice. Annually in March the townsmen assembled for the election of officers and to act upon any other matters which had been mentioned in the warrant for the meeting. This warrant, and only the matters stated in it could be considered, was issued by the selectmen, the actual directors of town affairs, to the constables who then "warned" or gave notice of the meet-

[45] Trumbull, *op. cit.*, II, 298.

ing. Actually only "the freeholders and other inhabitants rateable at twenty pounds estate" could vote in the election of the selectmen, constables, tithingmen, fence-viewers, hog-reeves, hay-wards and other town officers.

Generally the meeting was opened with prayer; then the warrant for the meeting was read, and a moderator or president was chosen. The town then proceeded to a choice of selectmen, from three to nine in number, and the minor town officers. At this meeting, or at others during the year, instructions would be drawn up to the representative of the town at the General Court.[46] The warrant for the Northampton town meeting on March 2, 1747, for example, called the freeholders together to elect the town and county officers, to consider the bills of credit which the town had at interest and to consider also the encroachment of various individuals on the private ways and meadows.[47]

The selectmen, as their name indicates, were men selected to manage town affairs. Their powers were very great and, while in theory a group of equals, they had a chairman, "the first selectman," who acted as leader and generally had more influence than his fellows on the board. These men were largely responsible for local financial administration, often determined and assessed town taxes, supervised the common wood and pasture land, let public contracts, sold town property, conducted town suits and regulated the admission of new members to the community. In short, they were to all intents and purposes practical dictators although ever restrained by the constant searching criticism of neighbors.[48]

Alongside the town government functioned a most important organization, the town proprietors. This group originated at Northampton in 1653 when the tract of land which was to be the site of the town was granted to several petitioners who sought to found a settlement for "the

[46] J. F. Sly, *Town Government in Massachusetts*, Ch. iv, *passim*.
[47] Northampton Town Records, March 2, 1747. Mass. Hist. Soc.
[48] Sly, *op. cit.*, Ch. ii. *passim*.

further inlarging of the territories of the Gospell of our Lord Jesus Christ And the common utility of the publick weale."[49] At first the group had been identical with the town as practically all the inhabitants at the time of settlement were proprietors, but this condition was changed with the passing of the years. When the settlement was being established, the proprietors parcelled the land among themselves for home lots, pasture and tillage. After laying out streets and highways, they set aside the remainder of the original grant as the "common and undivided lands." This remaining land was held under their exclusive control and only those who were proprietors could use it for pasture, tillage, or cutting timber.[50] As long as all the citizens were proprietors the system was free from criticism but when the proprietors gradually became a privileged class, antagonism appeared. The proprietors formed a close corporation consisting of the heirs of the original grantees and those whom they chose to admit to membership in common ownership. A man might possess a freehold but, unless the proprietors admitted him to their number, he was excluded from the "common and undivided lands."[51] Moreover the proprietors were independent, except of the General Court. Quite naturally the non-proprietors, when they had grown sufficiently in numbers and strength, rose against the proprietors in outraged protest.

Once a year the proprietors met to discuss and settle all questions relating to their lands; adjourned meetings were held almost monthly. The most important officer of their organization was the clerk who not only kept the records but appointed the place for meetings, notified the proprietors of these meetings, and unless a special agent were appointed acted at all times as their representative. Except that attention was focused on land problems, these gatherings were town meetings in miniature.[52]

[49] Trumbull, *op. cit.*, I, 5.
[50] R. H. Akagi, *The Town Proprietors of N. E. Colonies*, p. 3.
[51] *Ibid.*, p. 45.
[52] *Ibid.*, pp. 60-61.

# RIVER GOD 87

Joseph Hawley played an active part in both of these organizations. He first sat on the Northampton board of selectmen in 1747, when yet not twenty-four,[53] and with but two exceptions he was elected to the board regularly for thirty years. After ten years of apprenticeship he was chosen first selectman in 1761 and served the town in that office continuously until 1777. But before leading the board he had spent ten years in his father's old office of town clerk, recording in his broad penmanship the vital data of Northampton life as well as the minutes of the town meetings. In 1751, at the May meeting, Hawley acted as moderator for the first time and thus began presiding over town meetings as he was to continue doing until another generation had grown up.[54] His skill as a presiding officer was widely recognized and once when he was at the provincial capital, he was called to take charge of a Boston town meeting whose turbulence had overwhelmed the regular moderator.[55]

While much of his service to the town was in the office of selectman, he also worked on many special committees for the settlement of town problems. One of the most difficult and constant was that of the town lands. His first recorded contact with it was in 1749 when he acted on a committee to survey the highways and lots in the town land before a division of land among the inhabitants.[56] Three years later he was serving on a committee to consider selling parts of the town's highways and streets, and because the matter was not easily determined he acted in a similar

[53] Northampton Town Records, March 2, 1747. Mass. Hist. Soc.
[54] Judd Manuscript. Northampton Material, II, 28.
[55] Trumbull, *op. cit.*, II, 539. In 1766 the General Court sent Hawley to Great Barrington to act as moderator of its town meeting. *Mass. Acts and Resolves*, XVIII, 129.
[56] Northampton Town Records, I, Feb. 9, 1749. The Northampton Town Records are to be found at Northampton and in the collections of the Massachusetts Historical Society at Boston. These sets largely duplicate each other. Where the citation is to the material at Boston a special note is made.

capacity the next year.⁵⁷ In 1759 he was active looking up the town's title to lands in the meadows and in selling some of the land which had formerly been in the jail-yard.⁵⁸ Ten years later one Jonathan Clap claimed an abandoned county road as his own, but an investigation by Hawley and others showed this to be untrue. They recommended that the town either sell the land to Clap or bring suit to dispossess him.⁵⁹ A few years later Hawley was on a committee to investigate the encroachments on the town lands along Mill River.⁶⁰

Hawley's real contribution to the problem of landholding was in connection with the long-standing dispute over the "common and undivided lands." Periodically it had broken out with great bitterness splitting the town into two camps. Both the town and the proprietors claimed the right to make all land divisions.⁶¹ After many temporary compromises, which had momentarily ended the dispute, the town in 1754 reasserted its right to all undivided lands within its boundaries and, without so much as a by-your-leave, chose a committee to determine how this should be done.⁶² Now the dispute blazed up more fiercely than ever. For two years neither side could claim victory, but in 1756 the proprietors by a political manoeuvre found themselves on top.

At the town meeting that year a committee of eight was chosen to "concert some Terms of Settlement and accomodation of the long disputes and controversies between the Town of Northampton and those who claim the undivided lands of the Town."⁶³ At an adjourned meeting ten days later, Joseph Hawley who was a member of the committee and incidentally one of the proprietors, brought in a report

[57] *Ibid.*, I, March 2, 1752; Nov. 27, 1753.
[58] *Ibid.*, II, 62-65.
[59] *Ibid.*, Nov. 30, 1767. Mass. Hist. Soc.
[60] *Ibid.*, May 22, 1770. Mass. Hist. Soc.
[61] Akagi, *op. cit.*, p. 142.
[62] *Ibid.*, p. 143.
[63] Northampton Town Records. II, 22. March 16, 1756.

recommending that for ten years a part of the common lands, actually an area four miles square, should be reserved to the inhabitants of the town with the privilege of pasturage and the cutting of all timber except white pine. At the end of the period this land was to be quitclaimed to the proprietors while the rest of the common lands was to be released immediately to the proprietors without restriction.[64] After considerable debate the report was accepted, and the dispute which had distracted the town for three quarters of a century was settled. No wonder that the proprietors soon chose Hawley for their clerk and kept him in that important position for the succeeding seven years.[65]

With the growth of the town new communities appeared in the Northampton township and these soon began to clamor for release from leading-strings. Southampton was the first. By 1741 it had became large enough to maintain a church and minister, and twelve years later an act of the legislature set the parish apart as a separate town. This brought up questions between the parent and the offspring, particularly that of the division of the lands and funds held by Northampton. Southampton's claim to a proportionate share of the school funds was not settled until 1770, when under Hawley's chairmanship a committee decided against the younger town's pretensions.[66] Another settlement called Pascommuck or Easthampton grew up four or five miles from the center. By 1769 its people felt independent enough to have a church of their own and petitioned for the privilege of worshipping separately. In answer, Hawley and others were appointed to consider the situation.[67] Nothing was settled and as a result the petitioners within three years were asking to be set off as an independent town. Again Hawley was chairman of the committee which sat upon Easthampton affairs and which this time

[64] *Ibid.*, II, 23.
[65] Northampton Proprietors Records, 1757-1778, pp. 1-10.
[66] Northampton Town Records, II, 157. May 22, 1770.
[67] *Ibid.*, II, 155. March 30, 1770.

brought in a report recommending that the petition be granted.[68] The report was adopted in the Northampton town meeting but many years elapsed before an act of the General Court cut the ties between the two settlements.

Occasionally Hawley's committee work was of a more homely nature. In 1760 the town purchased a new meetinghouse bell, but within a year the bell was mysteriously broken. In a day when few men owned or carried watches the ringing of the village bell to mark the noon hour and nine o'clock curfew was one of the necessities of life; the breaking of the bell was almost a calamity. As a result the townsmen, highly incensed at the accident, appointed a committee of which Hawley was chairman to investigate and prosecute if it seemed desirable.[69] Much of this homely work revolved about the church. As the town grew in population a perennial problem was the need to reseat the meetinghouse, a problem whose settlement required the greatest tact. Generally Hawley was on the committees which arranged sittings.[70] In 1772 the children, who had long been the instigators of commotions during church services, were causing so much disturbance that Hawley was appointed with others to bring in a town bill which would end the confusion. As a result of their recommendations a system of patrolling the meeting house during worship was instituted.[71]

Almost from the beginning of his activity in town affairs Hawley had been interested in the schools. On January 10, 1749, he was appointed with his old teacher, Samuel Mather, to consider the "better regulating of Schools and education of youth." The two men advised that in cold weather two schools should be maintained, one for grammar school students, the other for more elementary pupils.[72]

[68] *Ibid.*, III, 10. March 21, 1773.
[69] *Ibid.*, II, 98. Aug. 31, 1761.
[70] *Ibid.*, March 6, 1749, March 4, 1754, and frequently thereafter.
[71] *Ibid.*, II, 3.
[72] Hawley Papers, I, 13.

While their recommendations were not carried out immediately, this action was the beginning of an improvement in the town's educational system. In 1759 a regular school committee was appointed which with the selectmen supervised the town's schools.[73] It made Hawley's continued interest more easy because as a selectman he was in constant association with the school committee and as the schoolmaster frequently lived in the Hawley household, there were close personal relations. Whenever Hawley was in Northampton he visited the center schools regularly, going to them directly after his semi-weekly shave.[74]

On one occasion his interest in education carried him beyond the Northampton schools. In 1762 Israel Williams attempted to found a college in western Massachusetts which would serve that section in the same manner as Harvard did the seaboard. Western Massachusetts then, even as now, had a degree of self-consciousness; what was more logical than the setting up of a college which would draw support from the rapidly growing river and hill towns? Harvard, it was felt, was far too distant as well as too expensive. Moreover, the orthodox westerners were not able to accept Harvard's less vigorous Calvinism. Probably the question of a western college had long been discussed in Hampshire County but matters did not come to a head until the beginning of 1762. At that time a bill was introduced in the General Court for the setting up of "Hopkins College" at either Northampton, Hadley or Hatfield. The bill named the trustees of the proposed college, among them the leading men of the county, Israel Williams, John Worthington, Oliver Partridge and Joseph Hawley.[75] The bill received a small majority in the House, but was defeated in the council. Shortly afterward a new

[73] Trumbull, *op. cit.*, II, 306.
[74] Notes of George Bancroft, Hawley Papers, I.
[75] Mass. Archives Literary, 1645-1774. LVIII, 459. Apparently in the first bill it was intended to name the college for Samuel Hopkins, the minister of Hadley and a nephew of Jonathan Edwards.

bill was introduced seeking a charter for "Queen's College" in Hampshire County but it met with the same fate as the first.[76]

This threat to Harvard aroused its overseers to immediate protest. Governor Bernard, acting on his own authority, had already signed a charter for the proposed Queen's College; the protests of the Harvard overseers caused him to withhold its delivery and ultimately to suppress it. Meanwhile letters were passing back and forth arousing opposition to the proposed college and a circular letter from the Harvard overseers to influential friends in England made certain that Queen's College would find little support there.

Oxenbridge Thacher wrote to a friend that what occasioned "the most gaping of late (we are not awake enough to speak) is a charter for a new college in the county of Hampshire. The monarch of the county [Williams] (you know it always was under regal government) took great offence at his son's being placed some years ago something lower in a class at our college than befitted the son of a King. He therefore, and his privy council came down the last Sessions prepared with a petition to incorporate a college in that county."[77] Thacher was not wholly just to Williams' motives, but letters like his as well as the formal protests from Harvard effectually prevented Joseph Hawley from ever acting as a trustee of Queen's College.

Time and added maturity, with possibly the shock of Elisha's death, won Hawley over from Arminianism and sometime in the late 1750's he returned, outwardly at least, to the orthodox fold. His piety and prominence in the community led in 1762 to his election as a deacon of the church, the highest ecclesiastical position which a layman

[76] J. Quincy, History of Harvard, II, 105. See also his appendices vii, viii, ix.

[77] A. L. Perry, *Origins in Williamstown*, p. 227. The author has an excellent brief discussion of this episode.

could hold in the congregational churches.[78] Some time after the election he accepted the honor and performed a deacon's duties until the end of his life. Tolerant towards others in religious matters, he became very strict in his own observance of religious forms. On one occasion, returning home from a journey, "the sun set upon a Saturday evening, when he was within a few miles of his home. He remained where he was until the sun set the next day, and then finished his journey."[79] Hawley was always interested in church singing and while not much of a singer himself was fond of music. The choristers often met at his house for practice, and he strove to see that the town's reputation for excellent church music was maintained.[80]

Throughout all these years of concern for public affairs, home life went on much as usual. In the summer Hawley and his wife rose at five o'clock and during the winter at six. Both then went to the barn and while he was feeding the stock, Mercy would milk their few cows. Afterward came morning prayer.[81] Sunday was a day devoted to religion. Dressed in homespun and a checked shirt of Mercy's making, Hawley rode to church on horseback, his devoted wife sitting behind him on a pillion.[82] On other days if there were hours of leisure, Hawley often browsed through the little library which he slowly built up. When works on law became tiresome, he could turn to such varied fare as Cato's *Letters or Essays on Liberty,* Thomas Hutchinson's still uncompleted *History of Massachusetts Bay,* or a volume of Thomas Gordon's attacks on the high church party in his *Independent Whig.* There were Samuel Butler's popular satire and attack on Puritanism, *Hudibras*—a volume which hardly seems to belong to the library of a Northampton deacon—and Pope's *Essay on Man,* somewhat

[78] Records of the First Church of Northampton, March 29, 1762.
[79] Hutchinson, *op. cit.,* III, 296.
[80] Trumbull, *op. cit.,* II, 531.
[81] Notes of George Bancroft, Hawley Papers, I.
[82] Judd Manuscript, I, 149.

advanced literature for eighteenth century rural Massachusetts. There was also Milton's *Paradise Regained* or *Samson Agonistes* to afford a good deal of pleasure.[83] For the serious moments he owned Flavel's *Works*, Sixe's *Divine Breathings* and Owen's *Sermons and Tracts*.[84] With these and the few books which he could borrow in the town, it was possible to stimulate some intellectual life even in the isolation of western Massachusetts.

There were no children to carry on the Hawley line, yet the household was seldom without the young faces of boys and girls who had been apprenticed to the Major and his wife. About 1763 the Hawleys adopted Joseph Clarke, Mercy's nephew, and during the succeeding years they lavished on him all the care and affection that would have been given to one of their own children.

In general it was a happy, simple life until in 1760 came the first foreboding of dark days; Hawley found himself a victim of the family taint of melancholia.[85] Was he too to be obsessed with the torturing fears to which his grandmother and father had been a prey? The spell passed but ever after a spectre was constantly hovering over the lives of Joseph Hawley and his beloved Mercy. In the fall of 1764 the overpowering depression returned again, and while it was still with him, Hawley wrote despairingly on the flyleaf of his copy of Johnson's dictionary:

This day is the ninth day of January A.D. 1765 and ever since Tuesday the Second day of October last I have been Incapacitated to Judge in moral or religious matters lost as to all the business of my Profession, To wit of the Law; the abovesd Second day of October was the last day as I remember I attempted to devise or give Counsel as a Lawyer and for part of that day I was capable But never since—I have been able Since and am yet able to deal a

[83] These works are to be found autographed by Hawley in the library of Miss Clara Hudson.
[84] These works are mentioned either in Hawley's will or among certain notes in the Hawley Papers, I, 77.
[85] Notes of George Bancroft, Hawley Papers, I.

little in figures, But lost as to all matters which are deemed matters of Judgement—my memory extremely broken—Embarrassed about Religion—all courage Spirit, motive or Spring of action or whatsoever it was which formerly animated me, and which now keep the world alive and in motion absolutely extinguished—O Piteous case

Joseph Hawley

No more prospect of being restored to my former State of enjoyment capacity for business, and other action than when a limb of the body is amputated, that another will grow out in its Stead. J. H.[86]

Yet the fit of gloom—mild insanity we would call it—gradually lightened; by spring Hawley was active again in town affairs, and in his profession. There were still years of work ahead, in spite of recurring fits of depression, the years during which he was to achieve fame and reputation throughout Massachusetts Bay. Already he was an outstanding figure in Hampshire County and men in Boston were calling him, along with Israel Williams and John Worthington, a "river god." Now the time had come when this "river god" must begin to play a more active and important rôle in the province.

[86] From the flyleaf of Johnson's *Dictionary* in the library of Miss Clara Hudson.

CHAPTER VI

## AT THE "PARLIAMENT OF MASSACHUSETTS BAY"

Joseph Hawley was now in the prime of life and about to attain the zenith of his career. Behind were the years of apprenticeship, the years of growth which had given him his secure place in the western part of the province. Rash and over-zealous at times, a good hater if not the complete partisan, he yet possessed a certain steadiness and soundness that won general confidence. In 1766 his fellow townsmen sent him as their representative to the General Court.[1] At the end of May, when the trees were gay with new foliage and the lilacs were blooming in the dooryards, he rode out of Northampton, crossed by ferry to Hadley, and took his way along the Bay Road towards Boston to begin a decade of political activity as the "Patrick Henry of Massachusetts."[2]

But Boston and the General Court were not new to him for he had served three terms there long before, and become familiar with the workings and form of government. The legislature, which convened every May at the Province House in King Street, was composed of two bodies, the house of representatives and the council. The members of the house, who represented the towns of the province, in their turn selected, with the retiring council and subject to the governor's veto, the twenty-eight members of the council. In the background was ever-present the shadow of the Crown, exercising the right to disallow laws, to appoint the governor, the lieutenant-governor and secre-

---

[1] He has been elected to represent Northampton in 1764 also but apparently never took his seat.
[2] T. C. Amory, *Life of James Sullivan*, I, 93.

tary; actually, through control of the purse, a good deal of the real power rested with the legislature, the Great and General Court. This control included not only the levying of taxes and appropriations of revenues, but even more important, the determination of the governor's salary, which was increased or not largely according to the whim of the legislature and the governor's behavior.[3]

For years this governmental system had creaked along. Legislative sessions were frequently enlivened by quarrels between the royal governor and the more democratic assembly; in 1766 these quarrels were entering the final phase that was to lead to revolution. In 1725 some of the chronic disputes had been temporarily settled by the issue of an "Explanatory Charter" which gave the governor the right to veto the assembly's choice of a speaker, but at the same time gave the house the right to adjourn from day to day without the governor's leave. This compromise, however, had not been wholly successful; the governor's rather frequent disapproval of the assembly's choice of a speaker as well as his veto of the choice of councillors was a constantly recurring irritant.

There were other points of friction which aided in creating uncomfortable relations between the representatives of the Crown and of the province. One of these was the long-continued opposition of the Lords of Trade to the erection of new towns because they feared the resulting growth in size of the house of representatives. Such a policy antagonized both settlers and land speculators. Periodically, also, there was strife over the meeting place of the General Court. While the charter was not specific, custom placed the sittings at Boston. Even so at many

[3] J. G. Palfrey, *History of New England*, III, 71-74. See also the Massachusetts Charter of 1691 and the Explanatory Charter of 1725 in *Mass. Acts and Resolves*, pp. 1-23. The following narrative is based to a large extent upon Edward Channing, *History of the United States*, III, pp. 29-81, J. T. Adams, *Revolutionary New England*, pp. 250-369, and A. M. Schlesinger, *Colonial Merchants, passim*.

times, usually to escape epidemics raging in Boston, the General Court met in other towns; whenever the governor wished to move the sittings to Cambridge or Roxbury he had some precedent with him. But there was the germ of a dispute in this question which, if linked with others more fundamental, such as the support of the governor from royal revenues, might well bring on a serious crisis.

For years one of the regular disputes in Massachusetts had been over the governor's salary. The Lords of Trade insisted that this should be fixed, but the provincial leaders saw early that one of the most effective means of maintaining provincial independence was by making royal officials "dependent upon the good will of the General Court." This could be done through granting money for salaries from time to time. One royal governor after another—Phips, Bellomont, Dudley, Shute, Burnet, and Belcher—found himself unable to secure a settled salary. At last the English government gave up the attempt and the Massachusetts General Court continued its policy of periodically voting a salary to the governor.

When Hawley first sat in the house of representatives in 1751, receiving considerable attention and "quite respect eno" for "one who is wholly a new member," there was little of this irritation. Governor William Shirley was too able and shrewd an executive to allow petty differences to mar his administration. Times changed, however, and by 1766 Shirley's place was filled by Francis Bernard, an unpopular, tactless, and obstinate "gentleman of third-rate abilities whom the pressure of a large and growing family" had sent to the colonies. Gifted with neither foresight nor hindsight, he early found himself entangled in disputes and controversies arising both from his own incompetence and the vagaries of imperial policy.

But there had been greater, more fundamental changes. By 1763 the struggle for a continent had been settled in favor of Great Britain; for the first time in their history the American colonies needed to give no thought to the French menace along the frontiers. The Treaty of Paris had given Quebec and the lands east of the Mississippi to the English, though the French foreign minister, Choiseul had prophesied that the treaty would mark a pyrrhic victory, ending in the loss to England of her American colonies. With the end of the war the colonists felt, perhaps more strongly than ever, a certain maturity and self-consciousness. Their very manner of living made for self-confidence; now it was accentuated by the removal of the French menace.

The increasing note of independence—an independence which was still perfectly loyal to His Majesty George III—accompanied other aspects of the social evolution. Politics tended to replace religion in general colonial interest and men were far more likely to be heard discussing political theory than theology. Yet even this growth of religious indifference made no more acceptable the frequently recurring rumour of the probable establishment of an American episcopate. The possibility stirred antagonism in nearly every mind.

Meanwhile the ministry at London had been considering the imperial system. In 1760, as a war measure, it had begun to enforce the collection of customs duties. The colonists were particularly alarmed lest this should include enforcement of the Sugar Act of 1733 which placed a duty of sixpence per gallon on all molasses imported into the northern colonies except from British plantations. Since molasses was essential for the manufacture of the rum on which a good deal of New England's prosperity rested, and since the British plantations could not supply the demand, the collection of this prohibitive duty meant ruin to a basic industry. Small wonder then, that the announcement of the plans to enforce the Sugar Act caused widespread alarm.

To aid in the collection of the duty on molasses, the officials sought writs of assistance—general search warrants which would permit the searching of any house or ship, the seizing or opening of goods. As the attempts to use the writs of assistance coincided with the death of George II, the customs collectors applied for new writs; the granting of these the Boston merchants now decided to oppose. The case came up for hearing in the Superior Court of Judicature in February, 1761. James Otis, who appeared for the merchants, made a strong impression by his vigorous arguments against the writs and for the rights of the colonists as men and Englishmen. Later Joseph Hawley was to copy the report of this argument in his "Commonplace Book." The incident stirred up considerable feeling but eventually the writs were granted. Had it not been for later events, the episode would probably have been forgotten.

The end of the war with France found Englishmen face to face with difficult and in some respects new problems. Of paramount importance was the great increase in the public debt with the resulting rise in taxes, particularly the land tax. Another problem was the need for larger garrisons in North America. Perhaps most difficult of all was the necessity for devising a policy for the administration of Canada and the western country. But this would only add to the burdens of the British unless some solution were devised. Why not shift part of this burden to the colonists? It seemed logical that the colonists should pay part of the cost of empire, although they already felt themselves overburdened with taxation.

The ministry in 1764 finally moved towards the carrying out of the idea of colonial taxation and an overhauling of the imperial system. As a part of this plan attempts were made to reinvigorate the extremely lax customs service and some time before the commanders of ships in America were given authority to seize vessels suspected of smuggling. An American Revenue Act was passed levying new and, in some instances, higher duties on silks, fine fabrics, molasses and wines, other than British. But in the case of molasses the duty was only half that levied by the Sugar Act of 1733. New enforcement regulations were enacted which would place colonial trade and navigation in a strait-jacket. Another clause of the new legislation required that the

## PARLIAMENT OF MASSACHUSETTS BAY

proceeds of the duties should be paid into the "Receipt of his Majesty's Exchequer." Did this clause mean that specie would be drained from America? The radicals in the agitation which soon sprang up believed or pretended to believe so. The news of the passage of this legislation brought general protests from the colonies, protests which denied the legality of levying taxes on an American "without the consent of his representative." But these protests received little attention at London and worse was to follow.

On March 22, 1765, George III gave his assent to the Stamp Act. Under its provisions duties were to be assessed on all legal and official documents, on newspapers and pamphlets, playing cards, dice and retail spirituous liquors. Violations were punishable by heavy fines and forfeitures, which might be collected through the admiralty courts in which jury trial did not prevail. The news of this latest piece of Parliamentary legislation awoke new and more vigorous protests in America.

The Massachusetts General Court contributed its portion by sending a circular letter to the other colonial assembles calling a congress to meet at New York in October to discuss the situation. At this congress the colonists adopted resolutions asserting the right to enjoy all the rights of Englishmen and especially the right not to be taxed except by their own consent or by the consent of their representatives. Meanwhile mobs in Boston and other colonial centers had visited the stamp distributors, destroying their property and forcing their resignations.

In Boston, Andrew Oliver, the stamp distributor for the province, had been hanged in effigy and a small structure which he was believed to be building for a stamp office had been destroyed. Soon afterwards the Boston mob had gathered again to attack the homes of two of the customs officers and especially that of Chief Justice Hutchinson. After gutting Hutchinson's beautiful residence and throwing the manuscript of his famous history into the muddy street, the mob attempted to tear down the dwelling. Lawlessness of a milder sort had occurred throughout the province. Joseph Hawley had good reason to know of the incident provoked by the Stamp Act at Great Barrington for in a few months he would have to plead before the Superior Court at Springfield for the leader of the Great Barrington rioters.

Agitation and rioting effectively nullified the Act. Courts were closed temporarily, and technically all papers issued contrary to the Stamp Act were null and void. But soon people began to resume the ordinary course of business without the cursed stamps. Meanwhile the disturbances had caused so much commercial distress that merchants nearly ceased importing. Englishmen at home were thrown out of employment, and petitions for repeal from English merchants, manufacturers and tradesmen were added to the colonial protests.

The changed scene had brought forth changed leaders. Since the decade of the fifties the house of representatives under the leadership of men like Samuel Adams and James Otis had definitely passed into the control of the anti-court or anti-government party. Whatever Adams' shortcomings may have been, none could gainsay his matchless manipulation of politics and his clever partisan pamphleteering. A radical and a democrat, he was the organizer of the opposition party. Otis, soon to show early traits of insanity, had considerable ability as a writer and orator, but was violent, erratic and self-centered. James Bowdoin who was the opposition leader in the council had been elected to that body in 1757. Until then it had always loyally supported the governor. Opposed to Bowdoin in the council was Thomas Hutchinson, chief justice of the province—a man of wealth, culture and ability, devoted to the welfare of the province but first of all a loyal and conservative subject of the Crown. Hawley knew them all, either through his profession or through his earlier service at the capital. Among other familiar faces at the General Court were those of John Worthington and Israel Williams, men who shared with Hawley the name of "river god." Worthington, the able and conservative political boss of Springfield, was soon to turn away in alarm at Hawley's radicalism. Between Israel Williams and Hawley there was no love lost: perhaps it was due to some unknown family feud; undoubtedly Hawley repented the part he had taken in the Edwards affair which Williams had done so much to stimulate; possibly the cousins had been rivals for too long in the life of Hampshire County. In any case, since the time of the last French and Indian War there had been a growing coolness between them which was now to culminate in bitter political antagonism. One can only surmise how great was the influence of this hostility to Williams in determining Hawley's political attitude.

During his first years of representing Northampton at the General Court, Joseph Hawley had a varied experience.[4] As a major of Hampshire County he naturally served on many committees concerned with military matters. It might be the recommendation, after a careful investigation, that Fort Pelham and Fort Shirley be abandoned, or the consideration of a petition for the support of officers at Fort Massachusetts.[5] At other times he was on committees to wait upon the Governor to learn the condition of the stores in the province arsenal or to inform Shirley of conditions among the troops at Chignecto.[6] When an expedition was setting out for Crown Point in 1756, Hawley was active in securing an adequate commissary for the troops and in making allowances for the soldiers on their homeward journey.[7]

Prepared by his legal training to contribute valuable knowledge in the shaping of legislation, he assisted in the framing of various bills affecting statute law. When the council sent down a bill regulating the transfer of real

[4] He had been a member in 1751-52, 1754-55, and in 1755-56.
[5] *Journal of Mass. House*, 1754, pp. 37, 89.
[6] *Ibid.*, 1755, pp. 198; 1756, p. 360.
[7] *Ibid.*, 1756, pp. 289, 362.

estate, Hawley was on the committee which took it under consideration.[8] At the same session he sat with a committee to amend a bill entitled: "An Act for better securing and rendering more effectual Grants and Donations to pious and charitable Uses," and to consider especially the statute of mortmain.[9] In the next General Court he aided in the preparation of a bill to alter the penalties for certain criminal cases and also to make certain the payment of costs and charges in criminal actions when the accused was acquitted.[10] Furthermore, in 1754 he examined all laws about to expire with a view to possible new legislation.[11]

Often he was busy with various aspects of taxation. For some reason or other, Hawley was usually a member of the committees which framed bills levying an excise on wines, tea, coffee and tropical fruits.[12] Even when not a member of the house, he acted on the committee which farmed out this excise in Hampshire County.[13] In the sessions of 1754 and 1755 he assisted in the drafting of a general "Supply and Tax-Bill."[14] When the province taxes seemed to fall too heavily on the poorer towns Hawley was one of those who investigated the resulting complaints and petitions.[15]

All this had been but training for the more important service of his maturity. Now he was to be one of the leaders in a political struggle and to have little time for the smaller details of legislative work. Acquainted with the leaders of the General Court, bringing with him to Boston the unquestioning support of his town and a large part of his county, he took his place in the assembly with all the assurance of the "river god" that he was. In his pocket

[8] *Ibid.*, 1754, p. 127.
[9] *Ibid.*, 1754, p. 127.
[10] *Ibid.*, 1756, p. 282.
[11] *Ibid.*, 1754, p. 9.
[12] *Ibid.*, 1754, pp. 18, 32, 105.
[13] *Mass. Acts and Resolves*, XV, 187, 372, 613, 661; XVI, 421.
[14] *Journal of Mass. House*, 1754, p. 34; 1755, p. 376.
[15] *Ibid.*, 1754, pp. 53, 59.

were the votes of most of the representatives of Hampshire; as Hawley voted so did they. Small wonder that the radicals hoped to win him to their side; circumstances greatly assisted them.

The legislative session in the spring of 1766 opened in an atmosphere of expectancy. The governor was certain to announce the repeal of the Stamp Act. All the colonies were still echoing with the protests against that unfortunate piece of imperial legislation. The memory was still green of the numerous riots, of the marching mobs, of tarring and feathering. But the riots and agitation together with the petitions of the English merchants had not been without effect; the Stamp Act had been repealed. The address of Governor Bernard at the opening of the sitting was singularly unfortunate. His first sentence announcing the repeal of the Stamp Act should have been his text, but instead he launched forth into an attack upon the people for the riots of the previous summer and upon the house of representatives for its irritating insistence upon electing men to the council who would not support the governor.[16] Perhaps its most unpleasant nominee had been James Otis, but there were others whom Bernard found no easier to stomach. The committee of eight which prepared the customary reply to the governor's address was headed by Otis who with Samuel Adams, Joseph Hawley and Thomas Cushing probably did most of the work.[17] These men throughout the next few years were together on all important committees. Otis usually drafted their reports, Cushing toned them down, Adams revised and polished them, while if necessary they were passed upon by Hawley whose opinion and influence soon became very powerful in the legislature.[18] The reply of the house to Bernard's address returned blow for blow and in good measure. Bernard was

[16] *Mass. State Papers*, p. 74.

[17] Otis's election both to the council and as speaker of the house had just been vetoed by the Governor.

[18] W. Tudor, *Life of James Otis*, p. 248.

attacked for his criticism of the house and of the people; his disagreement with the elections to the council, the representatives declared, came dangerously close to a "direct impeachment of the two Houses of high treason."[19] But this sort of controversy was not new; it had become chronic.

A few days later Bernard again appeared before the General Court to communicate the contents of a letter from General Conway, one of the Secretaries of State, who, acting upon resolves of the House of Commons, had suggested compensation to the victims of the Stamp Act disturbances. The governor, however, spoke of the recommendation as a requisition and urged that, as it was based upon resolves of the House of Commons, all discussion about complying with it should be omitted.[20] The over-touchy members of the house did not receive this address of the governor's without some protest. In their reply they promised to consider the recommendation, but the question was raised: "If the authority with which it is introduced should preclude all disputation about complying with it, we should like to know what freedom we have in the case."[21] Nothing was now lacking for a vigorous dispute.

June dragged along, and yet no action was taken on compensation until toward the end of the month when the house finally sent a report of their decision to Bernard. With a certain amount of irony, however unconscious, the message declared: "We are sensibly afflicted with the loss [the victims] have sustained, and have the greatest abhorrence of the madness and barbarity of those persons who were instruments of their sufferings. Nothing shall be omitted by us and our department, to bring the perpetrators of so horrid a fact to exemplary justice; and if it be in their power to a pecuniary restitution of all damages." But as it seemed an act of generosity to make up the losses, the house was doubtful if it had the power to charge such an

[19] *Mass. State Papers*, p. 76.
[20] *Ibid.*, p. 81.
[21] *Ibid.*, p. 90.

# PARLIAMENT OF MASSACHUSETTS BAY 107

expense to the people without their specific consent. Possibly this approval might be obtained if the entire question were left for the next sitting of the court.[22] Quite naturally Governor Bernard considered this answer an attempt to evade the issue; realizing that nothing could be accomplished for the moment, he prorogued the legislature.[23]

At the reassembling of the General Court in October the governor demanded that this time a positive answer be given to the recommendations from the Crown. Weeks of debate followed in which Hawley took a leading part. Behind his interest in the proposed compensation was the Stamp Act riot at Great Barrington. The Superior Court had passed sentence on Hawley's client in September, and as a result of the refusal of the court to entertain the plea of treason, he was in prison during the sitting of the legislature. But possibly there might yet be a way to secure his release.[24]

The reply of the house to the governor's opening speech was probably in large part the work of Hawley; at least he was chairman of the committee which prepared it. Observing that it was His Majesty's "pious and benevolent intention that not only a compensation should be made to the sufferers, in the late times, but also that a veil be drawn over every disgraceful scene, and to forgive and even to forget, the undutiful behavior of his subjects, in those unhappy times," the house was firmly of the opinion that an

[22] *Ibid.*, p. 94.
[23] Hutchinson, *op. cit.*, III, 157.
[24] *Ibid.*, III, 158. Hutchinson wrote, probably to William Bollan: "At the Superior Court for Berkshire one of his [Hawley's] clients was tried upon an appeal from the court of sessions, where he with divers others had been convicted of a riot under pretense of opposing the Stamp Act. Only one appealed & the fact being fully proved the jury could not avoid finding him guilty . . . it had such effect upon his lawyer, that he came down to the General-Court determined to oppose a compensation, unless not only they who had injured the persons compensated but all others guilty of riots since the first disorder occasioned by the Stamp Act Should be pardoned." Hutchinson Correspondence (NYPL), p. 98.

indemnity to the offenders was of equal importance with compensation to the sufferers. As a result a bill was framed entitled: "An Act for granting compensation to sufferers, and general pardon, indemnity and oblivion to the offenders, in the late times."[25] Inasmuch as the house at its earlier sitting had stated unequivocally that the guilty deserved exemplary punishment, there was logical ground for a charge of gross inconsistency. Of the debates on the bill we have no record, but it is certain that Joseph Hawley was definitely opposed to compensation unless it included a general amnesty. When the resolves of the House of Commons were cited as reason for making compensation, Hawley is said to have retorted: "The Parliament of Great Britain has no right to legislate for us." At this startling declaration, Otis is said to have risen, bowed to Hawley, and remarked: "He has gone farther than I myself have yet done in this House."[26] Such was the temper of the time.

Although before the convening of the General Court for its fall sitting many towns had voted in favor of compensation or had left the question to the discretion of their representatives, the bill framed by the court was submitted to the towns for action. Northampton considered the question at a town meeting over which Hawley presided on November 24, 1766. The citizens trimmed slightly when they voted: "That upon all matters that are or may be under the Consideration of... house of representatives during the present Session Their representative Should Act according to his best Judgment and discretion on hearing the debates thereon in that house."[27] Since Hawley's position on the bill was well known, this was hardly avoiding the issue. As a result of the action of the various towns the bill was enacted and secured the Governor's reluctant assent on December 6, 1766.

[25] *Mass. State Papers*, p. 97.
[26] W. V. Wells, *Life and Public Services of Samuel Adams*, I, 127. This story in detail is probably apocryphal, although remarks of that nature undoubtedly were made in the heat of discussion.
[27] Northampton Town Records, Nov. 24, 1766.

Accompanying the Act was a set of resolves drawn up by a committee under Hawley's direction. These explained that the house had granted compensation because of "a loyal and grateful regard to his Majesty's most mild and gracious recommendation. . . and under a full persuasion that the sufferers had no just claim or demand on the province; and that this compliance ought not hereafter to be drawn into a precedent."[28] Compensation was paid almost immediately, but when the law was reviewed by the Crown it was hastily disallowed as usurping the king's exclusive power of pardon and indemnity. However, by the time the news reached Massachusetts the money had been paid and nothing more was said by either side about the affair.[29]

An interesting postscript to the compensation act is a letter Thomas Hutchinson wrote to his friend Israel Williams.

I hear [he wrote] the House have passed the Bill for the compensation by 53 votes against 35. Some of the latter I am told would have voted for it without an indemnity. I think entirely as you do upon it *but beggars must not be choosers.* It is said by many of the House it would infallibly have passed last sitting if it had not been to the surprise of everybody prevented by Mr. Hawley. I have not the least doubt of his integrity but I am afraid he has conceived some prejudice against me which he is not sensible of any influence from. Some who were in the gallery told me he argued that the rioters who had been in error had a claim to favor as well as the sufferers the chief of whom was a person of unconstitutional principles and that one time or other he might make it appear, others understood him that in the view of the people I was such a person. I had rather this had been said of me by a great many of some other Counties than by a single person of the County of Hampshire especially by a man of Mr. Hawley's character. I do not intend to lose the favorable

---
[28] *Mass. State Papers,* p. 100.
[29] Hutchinson, *op. cit.,* III, 160.

opinion he once had of me and I doubt not that one time or other I shall convince him he is mistaken.[30]

Williams attributed Hawley's stand to the influence of Otis and the other radicals, although he said of his cousin, "if he is not distracted the devil is in him."[31] The older man, however much he may have disliked his Northampton rival, thought he knew him well and wrote to the chief justice: "He [Hawley] will soon recant of what he has injuriously uttered elsewhere, if his mind be not strangely blinded. His prejudices and Zeal are apt to hurry him into great excess and mistakes sometimes."[32]

The end of this quarrel found Hawley in poor health again and it was several months before he was capable of resuming his legislative duties. But in 1767, the General Court was quiet, recuperating from the excitement of the two previous years. Public opinion after the repeal of the Stamp Act was not ready to accept radical measures, and the left wing of the house of representatives had to be content with the age-old disputes over the constitutionality of executive actions. Two such discussions took place during the sitting of the court. The first in importance grew out of the Quartering Act passed by Parliament in 1765 which required the colonists to supply troops stationed among them with certain necessary utensils, with vinegar, salt, rum or beer, and pay part of the cost of transporting these troops within the colony or province.[33] As might be expected no provision was made by the Massachusetts General Court for carrying out the Act.

[30] Hutchinson to Israel Williams, Dec. 2, 1766. Hutchinson Correspondence, Vol. IV. Hutchinson wrote to Bollan on Nov. 22, 1766 that the act for compensation would have passed "if Mr. Hawley who always before had shown himself well disposed, had not strangely appeared in opposition, & carried divers others with him who have a great opinion of his understanding and integrity." Hutchinson Correspondence, I, 98.

[31] Williams to Hutchinson. Dec. 15, 1766. Hutchinson Correspondence, I, 102.

[32] *Ibid.*, Jan. 5, 1767. Mass. Archives, XXV, 140.

[33] Channing, *op. cit.*, III, 45. For the text of this act, see William MacDonald, *Select Charters*, p. 306.

## PARLIAMENT OF MASSACHUSETTS BAY 111

Late in 1766 an artillery company arrived at Boston and was garrisoned at the Castle in the harbor. As a result the house of representatives on the thirteenth of January coolly asked the governor if any provision had been made for these troops and if so by whom. Bernard at once admitted that he had made such provision, but with the consent of the council.[34] If one were looking for trouble, here was the occasion. Cushing, Otis, Hawley and Adams with three lesser lights were appointed a committee of the house to consider the question. Their report, embodied in a message to the governor, asserted that since the house alone possessed the power of originating, granting and disposing of taxes, the governor had acted unconstitutionally in providing for the troops on the authority of only the council. Certainly the house could hardly be expected to levy taxes for unauthorized expenses incurred by the governor.[35] The dispute dragged on for many weeks until it collapsed without a final decision.

In the other dispute, perhaps less fundamental, the house gained a decisive victory. Lieutenant-Governor Hutchinson had been a member of the council for several years, but in 1766, probably because of his unpopularity which had been growing for several years, he was not reëlected. Nevertheless, at the opening of the legislative session of 1767, he attended the first meetings of the council, claiming the right to do so because of his office as lieutenant-governor. This the house vigorously denied as unconstitutional because not specifically granted by the Charter. The reply to the governor's opening speech took up the issue and on March 3, 1767, Otis, Adams, Hawley and two others drew up a voluminous letter on the dispute to Denys De Berdt, the agent of the province in London.[36] As a result of continued pressure, the lieutenant-governor relinquished his claim and appeared no more at sittings of the

[34] *Mass. State Papers*, p. 105.
[35] *Ibid.*, p. 109.
[36] H. A. Cushing, *Writings of Samuel Adams*, I, 114.

council. Hutchinson attributed the opposition largely to Hawley's influence and recurring again to the case of the Stamp Act rioters, said of Hawley, perhaps rather unjustly: "He thought he had not been properly treated by the Lieutenant-governor as chief-justice in the Court of Common Law, and to revenge himself, brought the publick abuse against him [Hutchinson] in the assembly."[37]

If Hawley in the spring of 1767 thought he had not been well treated by the chief justice, he was to feel doubly so before the year was out. When the Superior Court sat at Springfield that fall, Hawley, it will be recalled, was stripped of his barrister's gown. Thomas Hutchinson thought the action generally approved of, but he failed to realize what its effects would be on a man of Hawley's disposition. Even the lieutenant-governor was aware that Massachusetts was not quiet. He protested against the "printed performances" of men like Hawley which "every Government under the sun would deem seditious."[38]

Perhaps Israel Williams saw the situation more clearly and was able to write with a certain mixture of truth and venom:

Some people are resolutely set to pursue plausible popular measures be the event what it will. I take my cousin Hawley to be one of that stamp. It is said by many he is honest, but under the influence of strong, irregular passions, which before he is aware may produce very bad effects. I expect it will be so, and his resentment not yet spent will appear very manifest when he gets to Court. If the judges of the Superior Court, are not out of his reach, they may expect retaliation for the supposed injury he has met with . . . he is much altered from what he was, is more haughty, self-sufficient obstinate and less disposed to suspect himself than formerly—owing I imagine to the flattery and applause he has below, which though he pretends to despise is fatally caught by it.[39]

[37] Hutchinson, *op. cit.*, III, 175.
[38] Hutchinson to Thomas Pownall (?) Nov. 10, 1767. Hutchinson Correspondence, I, 125.
[39] Williams to Hutchinson, Dec. 28, 1767. Hutchinson Correspondence, I, 137.

Hawley's resentment was not immediately apparent at the General Court but from that moment he never wavered in his support of the radical party. He became one of the "profligate abandoned fellows" as Hutchinson called them and the leading radical from the western part of the province. And the time was to come when he would have his revenge on the judges of the Superior Court.

When the year 1767 was drawing to a close, the house of representatives appointed a committee to take into consideration the state of the province, a committee which included Samuel Adams, Otis and Hawley. They dispatched a protest against the new legislation, the Townshend Acts, to the Earl of Shelburne, Secretary of the State for the Colonies. This protest pointed out the inexpediency of Parliamentary taxation as well as the existence of charter privileges.[40] With the passage of the Townshend Acts the British Government once again was trying to make its imperial system effective—this time by levying import duties on glass, lead, tea, painters' colors and paper, and worst of all, by establishing an American Board of Commissioners of Customs with headquarters at Boston. The revenue from these duties was to be used not only for the maintenance of the military forces in America, but where necessary for the support of civil government and the administration of justice. This last provision offered the opportunity for a new dispute which before long was seized by the radicals. The year's excitement was not confined to Massachusetts but spread through all the colonies. The protests and much of the agitation which three years before had accompanied the Stamp Act again burst forth.

The Massachusetts House of Representatives distinguished itself on February 11, 1768 by drawing up a circular letter to the other colonial assemblies, suggesting concerted opposition to the Townshend Acts by petition and discussion. At the same time addresses were voted to the king, the provincial agent, and Lord Shelburne who

[40] Cushing, *Writings of S. Adams*, I, 153.

had recently handed colonial affairs over to the Earl of Hillsborough. This circular letter and the addresses were the work of the inner circle, Cushing, Otis, Adams, and Hawley with a new member, John Hancock.[41] Both in England and America the circular letter caused a great commotion. One of Lord Hillsborough's first acts in his new office was to demand that the Massachusetts House should rescind its actions. But the house by a vote of 92 to 17 refused.[42] Governor Bernard acting on orders from Hillsborough at once dissolved the assembly. But before the General Court was dissolved Hawley with others was appointed to determine to what extent the royal naval and military forces were being used to enforce the revenue laws.[43]

Soon after the representatives had been sent home, the selectmen of Boston, undoubtedly under Samuel Adams' direction, requested the towns of the province to choose delegates for a convention at Boston. This body, it was hoped, would both consider the situation and act, incidentally, as an extra-legal body in the place of the legislature. Northampton considered the summons at a town meeting held on September 21, 1768. Although Hawley was moderator, the town did not accept the suggestion.[44] Perhaps in some things he could not go as far as his Boston colleague.

One of the refreshing things about Joseph Hawley was his ability in letters to his wife to break away from public affairs and think only of the homely problems of everyday life. Many of these little notes were written in the midst of the stirring times at Boston, in one instance, the day before the seizure of John Hancock's sloop Liberty for alleged smuggling was to start the mobs marching and rioting again.

[41] *Mass. State Papers*, p. 134.
[42] Channing, *op. cit.*, III, 99.
[43] *Journal of Mass. House*, 1768, p. 63.
[44] Trumbull, *op. cit.*, II, 326.

Boston June 9th 1768.

My Dear

I begin to look homeward somewhat wishfully but all I can say of that matter is that I shall not stay here a minute longer than is absolutely necessary. I send stuff for your [hood], suppose it must suit and be agreeable, for it was chosen by Mrs. Sally Hill, who is the very Tip of Taste. Mrs. Baxter [a relative] also concerned it and I also judge it will answer. I send two pounds of tea one for Mr. Stoddard [his cousin], one for ourselves—you will send Mr. Stoddard's without delay for they were most out when I came way. Encourage Joseph [his adopted son] to Diligence in his studys. My compliments all friends—and I remain your best Friend

J. Hawley[45]

During all these years in the midst of excitements, crucial debates, and political manoeuvres, Hawley's thoughts were always turning to Mercy, his "dear Child" as he generally called her, and to his beloved Northampton. Whatever happened his first loyalty was to Mercy and his home; she and his fellow townsmen remained his supporters to the end.

[45] Joseph Hawley to Mercy Hawley. June 9, 1768. Hawley Papers, I. The picture of this staunch Son of Liberty drinking tea in spite of the Townshend Acts and all the agitation against them is at least human.

CHAPTER VII

THE SONS OF LIBERTY

The struggle between Governor Bernard and the General Court reached a crisis in 1769, a year of non-importation with attendant boycotts, and more tarring and feathering. This controversy, the last in a long series between Bernard and the legislature, arose from the presence of troops in Boston.

The riots which had been stimulated by the seizure of Hancock's sloop Liberty had brought a request from Bernard for the sending of troops to Boston. After many delays the soldiers began to arrive in the fall of 1768 and were quartered in the town. The Quartering Act obliged each colony to provide barracks for the regular soldiers stationed in it, and only when the barracks were filled could the troops be billeted in taverns or stables. Inasmuch as there were barracks for two thousand men on an island in Boston harbor, the General Court could see no reason for providing quarters for them in the town; moreover to station them on the island would defeat the purpose of their coming. In the face of legislative opposition Bernard kept the soldiers in Boston, some on the Common, some in Faneuil Hall, and some in the Province House. There they remained while the General Court stubbornly refused to make any provision for their support and the commissary whom Bernard had appointed was in considerable doubt whether the supplies he obtained would ever be paid for.[1]

When the house of representatives met on May 31, 1769, it sent Bernard a protest against the presence of troops in Boston and demanded that the governor with-

---

[1] Channing, *op. cit.*, III, 96-97.

## THE SONS OF LIBERTY

draw them. This message, reported by the house leaders, Otis, Cushing, Adams and Hawley, asserted "that an armament by sea and land, investing this metropolis, and a military guard, with cannon pointed at the very door of the state house, where this Assembly is held, is inconsistent with that dignity, as well as that freedom, with which we have a right to deliberate, consult and determine."[2] Bernard was stirred to a prompt and brusque reply, declaring that he had no authority over the king's troops or ships, that he could give them no orders.[3] But, as the governor must have known, the house leaders were not likely to accept an answer of that nature. In a second message the house insisted that Bernard, as the king's lieutenant, must have the power to remove the troops. If he refused to do so, the house must have recourse to the only remaining remedy for an oppressed people, to "unite in laying their fervent and humble petition before their gracious Sovereign."[4] Bernard, seeking a way out of his difficulties and perhaps hoping to weaken the influence of the town of Boston on the General Court, took the legislature away from the troops by adjourning it to Cambridge. This act led almost directly to the petition from the General Court to the king on June 27, 1769, calling for Bernard's removal from the governorship.[5]

There were to be a few more exchanges before the governor's departure. Early in July the governor twice asked that some provision be made for the troops, particularly those barracked on Castle Island, and that the house should vote the necessary funds. These requests were based on the Quartering Act, which had already caused disputes between Bernard and the house. The answer, framed like so many by Otis, Hawley and Adams, refused absolutely to make any appropriation for the troops and

[2] *Mass. State Papers*, p. 166.
[3] *Ibid.*, p. 168.
[4] *Ibid.*, p. 188.
[5] *Ibid.*, p. 184.

condemned the act of Parliament as an infringement of chartered privileges, "for, in effect, the yet free Representatives of the free Assemblies of North America, are called upon to repay, of their own and their constituents money, such sum or sums, as persons over whom they have no check or control, may be pleased to expend."[6] In the debate at this time Hawley, who a short time before had declined election to the council, "made a publick declaration in the House, that he knew not how Parliament could have acquired a right of legislation over the colonies."[7] As a result of this uncompromising attitude, Governor Bernard prorogued the assembly.

Meanwhile, the province was being agitated by the possibility of the establishment of an Anglican episcopate. While there was no thought of it in England, demagogues like Samuel Adams stirred up considerable feeling over the issue. It only added to the year's excitement for, at the same time, merchants were being forced to sign the non-importation agreements now circulating. A refusal to sign was only too likely to lead to tar and feathers or the destruction of business.

In the fall Hawley was restored to his old position at the bar of the Superior Court, and Hutchinson wrote hopefully to Israel Williams: "Will there be no . . . reconciling Major Hawley? He can do a great deal of good or hurt as he happens to engage."[8] But the Hatfield "monarch" knew Hawley better, and in the height of his disgust wrote, he is "as unstable as water . . . there is no trust and dependence upon him."[9] Events were moving rapidly now, and Hawley, as Hutchinson was to learn, could not be reconciled.

[6] *Ibid.*, p. 184.

[7] Hutchinson, *op. cit.*, III, 264.

[8] Hutchinson to Williams, Sept. 18, 1769. Hutchinson Correspondence, Vol. IV.

[9] Williams to Hutchinson. Nov. 20, 1769. Hutchinson Correspondence, Vol. II.

## THE SONS OF LIBERTY 119

There was no mourning when Francis Bernard put out to sea on July 31, 1769, but joyous pealing of bells and firing of cannon; perhaps Bernard himself was secretly glad to shake the Massachusetts dust from his feet. Behind him, the lieutenant-governor, Thomas Hutchinson, was left to face the impossible situation in Massachusetts Bay. The General Court was scheduled to meet at Boston on January 10, 1770, but Hutchinson, acting on orders from the Crown, prorogued it to meet at Cambridge on the following fifteenth of March.[10] Before the Court met the Townshend Duties, with the exception of the duty on tea, were repealed; prosperity was returning to the province, and it seemed that possibly the worst was over.

The troops against whom the assembly protested so vigorously but vainly at the preceding session, were still in Boston, constantly harassed, insulted and tormented by the town toughs. On March 5, there was a clash in King Street which at last brought about their removal. With the "Boston Massacre" fresh in mind the General Court convened at Cambridge. "From this time," the lieutenant-governor declared, "Mr. Samuel Adams may be considered the most active member in the House. Mr. Hawley, member for Northampton, was equally, and perhaps more, attended to ; but Mr. Adams was more assiduous, and very politically proposed such measures only, as he was well assured Mr. Hawley would join in."[11] The House in its reply to Hutchinson's opening address protested against the forced meeting of the Court at Cambridge, but the lieutenant-governor was adamant. Accordingly on March 24, 1770, a committee of nine, including Cushing, Adams, Hawley and Hancock was appointed to "consider the state of the Province and to inquire into public grievances."[12] It was the beginning of a continuous dispute

[10] *Mass. State Papers*, p. 194.
[11] Hutchinson, *op. cit.*, III, 293.
[12] *Mass. State Papers*, p. 201.

against meeting in Cambridge that lasted, in spite of frequent prorogations, throughout the year.

The general situation is described in a letter Joseph Hawley wrote home:

> You will Perceive, [he said] by the Papers that the Council and house are very uneasy at the Court's being held at Cambridge. It was sometime before they would Consent to enter on business but on Saturday the 24th of March, after Protesting against the abuse and grievance of the Court's being moved from the Seat of Government they applied themselves closely to business, of which there is much to do, but we daily find ourselves retarded by reason of our distance from the Province records and for want of convenient places for Committees to Sit in etc. etc. The House has sent home a full representation of the late Massacre at Boston. The Troops are at Castle Island, and the Town of Boston are determined never to suffer them to return. . . . As to my return home I am not able at present to fix any time, when it is probable. We are in dayly expectation of news from England, and when that comes we shall be able to judge better of the rising of the assembly. I shall return as soon as possible Consistent with my Duty, for I long to be at home. The Lt. Gov. treats the house with great Complaisance, as I expected he would. . . .[13]

The assembly's protests against meeting in Cambridge continued as the session dragged on; in the end it spelled a year without accomplishment.

Matters seemed at stalemate, and conservatives hoped that there might yet be a way out. Behind the scenes the radicals may have been working, but on the surface order appeared to have returned. When the General Court convened in April, 1771, Hutchinson announced that he had been appointed governor. He insisted that the Court continue its meetings at Cambridge, and so the old stupid dispute was renewed. The new governor, unhappy in his post, realized that he could not expect any great regard from the house while the Boston men were

[13] Hawley to Mercy Hawley, April 3, 1770. Hawley Papers, I.

## THE SONS OF LIBERTY

supported by so influential a member as Hawley.[14] Rather pathetically he wrote to Israel Williams: "I think sometimes that one man [Hawley] from your neighborhood can never say the Lords Prayer, for if I had really trespassed against him, as I don't know that I ever did, he knows that the restitution made to his place, was owing to me and he ought to have forgiven me upon meer moral as well as Christian Principles."[15] Yet Hutchinson must have known that Hawley's support was irretrievably lost. Legislative protests, however, were less vigorous than in the previous year and the session proved uneventful. During much of the time Hawley was in the western part of the province, and so was absent from Boston.

One weapon in the hands of the legislature against the executive had always been control of the governor's salary and the annual appropriations. Should this power be taken from the General Court, the government might easily become too powerful a representative of the Crown. Small wonder then that a tempest broke in 1772, when the governor admitted that, as the Townshend Acts had provided, his salary was being paid by the Crown. Suspected for some time, it immediately became an issue with the legislators. A house committee under Hawley's chairmanship drew up a set of resolves attacking royal support of the governor and contending that any provision for his salary except through grants and acts of the assembly was an infringement of the charter and unconstitutional. This dangerous innovation seemed to violate the provision that the General Court should levy taxes for the support of the government. The governor was certainly an important part of the system. Royal payment of the executive would destroy the essential checks and balances of the government and thus would be

[14] Hutchinson to Williams. April 1, 1771. Hutchinson Corresponddence, Vol. IV.
[15] Hutchinson to Williams. April 6, 1771. *Ibid.*, Vol. I.

an "important change of the constitution."[16] Thomas Hutchinson described this report drawn up by Hawley as "well adapted to the purpose of inducing the people to believe that their rights by Charter were invaded, and that the powers, which in all free governments, ought always to remain in the people, were, by this act of the King, taken from them."[17]

When the governor a few days later asked the House to make some necessary repairs to the Province House where he was residing, Hawley framed a reply refusing to do so while the building was occupied by a governor receiving outside support. Whatever may have been Hawley's former feelings towards Hutchinson, he now could see little good in him and wrote home: "I think our Governor is bereft. You see by the Papers how he acts."[18]

In the midst of all these controversies the Boston *Gazette* printed an extract purporting to be taken from a London paper. Some wag saw the struggle in the General Court as a drama with the radicals and conservatives as the players. So in the form of a theatrical notice the story ran:

Tomorrow, by permission of the Right Honorable the Earl of Hillsborough will be performed at Cambridge in New England The Modern Farce of Legislation, by the Members of the General Assembly, or Parliament of Massachusetts Bay in America, who (by ministerial proclamation) are then and there to meet for Dispatch of divers weighty, great and seemingly important matters of State. The principal Characters are,

| Mr. Hutchinson | Mr. Ruggles | Mr. Adams |
| Mr. Oliver | Mr. Flucker | Mr. Cushing |
| Mr. Russell | Mr. Otis | Mr. Hawley |
| Mr. Bliss | Mr. Hancock | Mr. Dexter |
| Madame Brattle | Mrs. Gray and others[19] | |

---

[16] *Mass. State Papers*, pp. 325-29.
[17] Hutchinson, *op. cit.*, III, 357.
[18] J. Hawley to Mercy Hawley. June 8, 1772. Hawley Papers, I.
[19] Boston *Gazette*, August 31, 1772. The Massachusetts General Court may never have called itself the "Parliament of Massachusetts Bay," but the house of representatives claimed the status of the British House of Commons. See *Mass. State Papers*, pp. 246, 297.

## THE SONS OF LIBERTY 123

As the year drew to a close the conservatives and particularly the governor were alarmed at the action of the various town-meetings throughout the province which, stirred up by the Boston committee of correspondence, were presenting their grievances in terms which seemed to question directly the right of Parliament to legislate for the colonies. For a long time Hutchinson had been trying to avoid any open dispute over the supremacy of Parliament, but now he came to feel that a stand must be made. At the opening of the General Court on January 6, 1773, he delivered an able speech which asserted the authority of Parliament over the American colonies.[20] The message came as a great surprise to all parties and, being widely printed in the provincial papers, caused general discussion. Not until the twenty-sixth of the month did the House reply, but then they sent one of the most able documents produced by the radicals up to that time. A careful attempt was made to refute the governor's position. With many references to English history and provincial documents, it was contended that the king had never regarded the colonies as being under Parliament. Citations from Hutchinson's own *History of Massachusetts Bay* were used to show that the founders of the colony had likewise never regarded Parliament in the light of supreme law-giver. The house declared that "when our predecessors first took possession of this plantation or colony, by a grant and charter from the Crown of England, it *was not* and never had been the sense of the kingdom, that they were to remain subject to the supreme authority of Parliament." Furthermore, the message continued, if there had been any instances of submission to the acts of the august assemblage at Westminster, it was because of "inconsideration, or a reluctance at the idea of contending with the parent state," not because of "a conviction or acknowledgement of the Supreme Legislative authority of Parliament." To clinch the argument the message concluded: "These are

[20] Hutchinson, *op. cit.*, III, 371.

great and profound questions. It is the grief of the House, that, by the ill policy of a late injudicious administration America has been driven to the contemplations of them, and we cannot but express our concern, that your Excellency, by your speech, has reduced us to the unhappy alternative, either of appearing by our silence to acquiesce in your Excellency's sentiments, or of thus freely discussing the point."[21] Yet Samuel Adams had long been waiting for the opportunity to open such a discussion.[22]

Who drew up this message? Samuel Adams, John Hancock and Joseph Hawley were the three prominent names on the committee which reported it and Adams' eulogistic biographer has claimed the authorship for his hero.[23] Thomas Hutchinson said later: "Mr. Hawley and Mr. Samuel Adams were the persons who had the greatest share in preparing it, being assisted by Mr. John Adams, who was not at this time a member [of the House], but whose character, as a man of strong natural powers and of good knowledge in the laws, was established."[24] Hawley insisted that the committee should seek the advice and opinion of John Adams on every question. As no action upon legal and constitutional subjects could be carried "without the concurrence and support of Major Hawley" the committee gracefully submitted.[25] Probably the truth is that the message was a joint work in which Joseph Hawley along with the Adamses had a large and important share. How these three men worked together is shown by a letter from Samuel Adams to John Adams on Feb. 22, 1773, asking for advice on a legal point. He wrote: "I am sorry to trouble you . . . but to tell you a Secret, if there be a lawyer in the house in Major Hawley's Absence, there is no one I incline to confide in."[26]

[21] *Mass. State Papers*, p. 351-64.
[22] Wells, *op. cit.*, II, 29.
[23] *Ibid.*, II, 31.
[24] Hutchinson, *op. cit.*, III, 374.
[25] *Works of J. Adams, op. cit.*, II, 311.
[26] Cushing, *Writings of S. Adams*, III, 430.

The weight of history was probably with the governor in this new dispute, but his had been a bad move strategically.[27] For a long time the radicals had waited to open the question of parliamentary supremacy, although hesitating to take the first step. Now the issue was rasied and through the length and breadth of the Province it was debated at firesides and across tavern tables. Thomas Hutchinson, staunch but blind royalist that he was, scoffed at the answers of the General Court. He wrote to his predecessor: "The papers I enclose will shew what we are about ... You will think they [the Council and House] have made miserable work of it and yet you have the utmost effort of Bowdoin's genius in one House, and Hawley's and Adams' in the other. What will parliament say to this?"[28] Whether the king's lieutenant realized it or not, the situation was fast becoming acute, and what the radicals considered his irritating condescension was making it more so.

Hawley left Boston in late winter on the uncomfortable trip to Northampton. With the coming of spring he was one of the Massachusetts commissioners who met a New York commission at Hartford on the twelfth of May for the settlement of a long-standing boundary dispute between the two provinces. The previous year an agreement had been reached between them for the appointment of these delegations who with the two governors were to fix the boundary. Their decision was to be final and was not to be submitted to the provincial assemblies for approval or ratification. The New York men were particularly anxious that Massachusetts should withdraw the claim, based on the sea-to-sea clause in its old charter, for territory west of the Mohawk valley. Governor Hutchinson op-

[27] For a discussion of the supremacy of Parliament see R. L. Schuyler, *Parliament and the British Empire*. Also R. G. Adams, *Political Ideas of the American Revolution* and C. H. McIlwain, *The American Revolution*.

[28] Hutchinson to Bernard. Feb. 23, 1773. Hutchinson Correspondence, Vol. III.

posed relinquishing this claim and largely through his influence the New Yorkers withdrew their demand; the Massachusetts claim was not to be surrendered for another decade. Although Governor Hutchinson believed that the favorable outcome for Massachusetts was to a considerable extent the result of his presence, he admitted that "the weight of the business lay upon Mr. Hawley."[29] The satisfactory settlement gained no popularity for the governor nor did their working together renew the bonds of sympathy between him and Hawley.

When the commissioners returned to Boston in the latter part of May they found the town humming with rumors of treasonable letters from high provincial officials to the government at home. By the time the General Court convened on the twenty-sixth, public curiosity and excitement were at their height.[30] As soon as a committee of correspondence had been elected—a committee which included Samuel Adams, John Hancock, James Warren, Elbridge Gerry and Joseph Hawley—the word went around that within forty-eight hours an important disclosure would be made. In accordance with this prophecy Samuel Adams rose two days later in the House, asked that the galleries be cleared, and then read a series of letters from Hutchinson, Andrew Oliver, and others to a member of Parliament.[31]

Somehow Benjamin Franklin, the agent of the province, had obtained the letters in London and sent them under an injunction of secrecy to Thomas Cushing, the speaker of the Massachusetts House. Their contents were not particularly startling unless craftily edited and most of them were private, not official, correspondence. For some time the inner circle had known of the letters but Franklin's demand for secrecy had made them hesitate to lay them before the House. John Adams, writing about them in

---

[29] *Ibid.*, III, 391.
[30] *Ibid.*, III, 395.
[31] *Mass. State Papers*, p. 402.

his diary on April 24 of that year, commented: "Mr. Hancock is deeply affected; is determined in conjunction with Major Hawley, to watch the vile serpent [Hutchinson]."[32]

Hawley, that all-important member from Hampshire, was a member of the committee which was immediately appointed to consider the letters and to communicate with the Governor. Hutchinson for his part insisted that any letters he might have written contained only expressions which he had used frequently in his messages and speeches to the General Court.[33] Ultimately, when it became known that copies of the letters were circulating outside the House, Hawley obtained permission from Samuel Adams to publish them.[34]

Before the letters were printed, however, the resolves with the comments of the House upon them were published and circulated. The resolves, as was intended, aroused still further excitement. This was especially true of the resolve protesting against the conduct of Governor Hutchinson and Lieutenant-Governor Oliver and praying that the king "would be pleased to remove them forever from power in the province." One need not be surprised to find Hawley's name on the committee which prepared this petition to the king.[35] From any standpoint, the entire episode of the letters was discreditable. It effectively ruined Hutchinson's position in the Province, and from the backfire Franklin lost all influence with the British government. Probably he found small consolation in Samuel Cooper's letter from Massachusetts assuring him that "the Speaker and many others in the House are your steady friends, particularly Major Hawley, from Northampton, a gentleman of the law, who speaks with uncommon clearness and force, and is behind no man there in point of in-

[32] *Works of J. Adams*, II, 318.
[33] *Mass. State Papers*, p. 404.
[34] *Journal of Mass. House*, 1773, pp. 43-44.
[35] Boston *Gazette*, June 21, 1773.

fluence."[36] When the storm had begun to subside the house turned to the question of royal payment of salaries to judges, a new phase of the problem of royal control. Hutchinson met this situation by proroguing the General Court, hoping against hope that he would never have to meet it again.[37]

In spite of continued prorogations of the legislature the radicals maintained their organization. Behind the scenes many letters must have gone back and forth between Hawley and the Adamses, Bowdoin and Hancock. Samuel Adams wrote to Hawley that the British ministry could not be trusted and that he, at least, was certain that the right of imperial legislation and taxation would be maintained. "The Safety of the Americans in my humble opinion," he wrote, "depends upon their pursuing their wise Plan of Union in Principle and Conduct." Nevertheless any new steps should be taken warily, for "I am apprehensive that Endeavors will be used to draw us into an incautious mode of Conduct which will be construed as in Effect receding from the Claim of Rights of which we have hitherto been justly so tenacious."[38] Similar exchanges of idea and opinions must have been carried regularly in the postboxes of Massachusetts during all these years.

If Hawley ever reviewed in his mind the terms he had served in the General Court, he must have realized that he had been associated with very little constructive work. Most of his energies had been expended in the struggle with the governor; for the rest he had mainly devoted himself to routine bills and special acts of a minor importance. As in his first period of legislative work he had helped to draft the annual appropriation bills, both the bills of "supply" and of "ways."[39] In or out of the General Court

[36] J. Sparks, *Works of Benjamin Franklin*, VIII, 89.
[37] Hutchinson, *op. cit.*, III, 412.
[38] S. Adams to Hawley, Oct. 4, 13, 1773. H. A. Cushing, *Writings of S. Adams*, III, 52, 58.
[39] *Journal of the Mass. House*, 1776, p. 40; 1768, p. 14; 1770, pp. 92, 125.

## THE SONS OF LIBERTY

Hawley had long been connected with problems related to the unsettled and unapportioned lands of Massachusetts.[40] It was natural then for him to be on the committees concerned with the various phases of that problem. In 1766 he helped to prepare a bill taxing these unimproved lands and in the same General Court was concerned with the possible sale of such lands if the taxes on them remained unpaid.[41] Two years later he was one of those selected to examine the claims of certain individuals to the lands lying between the Saco River and the New Hampshire border.[42] In 1771, when royal opposition to the setting up of new towns had relaxed, Hawley brought in a bill for the incorporation of two towns in Berkshire County.[43] Frequently special bills were referred to Hawley, as for example, in the case of one James Sheppard who petitioned for the right to sell lands held by him as the guardian of a minor. The petition was granted provided he met the committee's requirement of giving a sufficient bond to the Judge of Probate in his county.[44] Again, Hawley helped Stephen Sewall, Professor of Oriental Languages at Harvard, to secure a legislative grant of £30 to supplement his regular salary.[45] When a petition—hopeless from the start—was introduced into the legislature to prohibit the importation of negro slaves into Massachusetts, Hawley sat with those who considered the matter.[46]

Perhaps one of the most interesting phases of Hawley's legislative career, apart from his preoccupation with the anti-government party, was his support of the movement to break down the alliance of church and state. After all, it is not surprising that the man who had led in the Edwards affair, and who had even temporarily accepted the more

[40] *Mass. Acts and Resolves*, XVI, 392, 482.
[41] *Journal of Mass. House*, 1766, pp. 110, 237.
[42] *Ibid.*, 1768, p. 12.
[43] *Ibid.*, 1771, pp. 23, 24, 114.
[44] *Ibid.*, 1771, p. 138.
[45] *Ibid.*, 1767, p. 135.
[46] *Ibid.*, 1766, p. 358.

liberal views of the Arminians should be active in the movement against the established church. Probably his position was largely the result of his sense of justice, of fair play. Besides, even with his own rigorous standards of piety, he was no blind follower of the clergy. At the time of his disbarment in 1767, when some of the clergy had sided against him, he had written: "Whatever reverence and submission may be due to the decrees and decisions of the Clergy on points and doctrines purely Theological, yet I have never seen any reason to suspect that they are blessed with infallibility on law cases and matters of a civil and political nature."[47] Possibly also he was easily attracted to causes which tended to upset established conditions.

Though throughout his public life Joseph Hawley stood for religious freedom, it is not always easy to trace his part in the long, drawn-out struggle. The Massachusetts Charter of 1691 granted religious toleration to all Protestants, but this did not prevent the Congregationalists, who were numerically the largest sect in the province, from passing laws to maintain their churches. Early in the eighteenth century the Quakers successfully resisted the payment of taxes for the support of the Congregational church, and in the next decades both Anglicans and Baptists secured the passage of legislation which in certain instances granted them exemption from religious rates.[48] In 1753 a law was enacted which exempted from the payment of a church tax all who could prove membership in a Baptist communion. But the means of proof were complicated and often expensive. The new law, therefore, proved most distasteful to the Baptists. Probably a part of the agitation which immediately arose was a petition

[47] Boston *Evening Post*, Jan. 11, 1768. A manuscript copy is in the Hawley Papers I.

[48] For a reasonably full discussion of this entire subject, see J. C. Meyer, Jr., *Church and State in Massachusetts from 1749-1833;* also S. M. Reed, *Church and State in Massachusetts, 1691-1740.*

to the General Court in 1754 from one Ebenezer Wadsworth who was seeking relief from punishment for not supporting a ministry which he did not attend. Hawley was one of the members of the house to whom the petition was referred, and while apparently no report was ever made, this was the beginning of Hawley's association with the Baptist problem.[49]

In 1758, when all the existing legislation expired, a new law was passed which permitted exemption in certain circumstances to both Quakers and Baptists. Membership had to be proved by the presentation of certificates. These were not always easy to obtain, while in any case attendance at some church was made compulsory. If Baptists or Quakers lived too far from their own churches, they were required to attend the nearest Congregational church and to pay for its support. This law was in force until 1771.[50]

During the 1760's at Ashfield, a new town in Hampshire County not far from Northampton, a notable case of Baptist persecution occurred. Although complicated by other issues, the essential point was whether or not the Baptists were exempt from contributing to the support of the Congregational ministry in the town. In the midst of petition and counter-petition to the legislature, Israel Williams pushed through the General Court a new law empowering the proprietors of Ashfield to levy and collect all taxes. This legislation was aimed directly at the Baptists because the proprietors as Congregationalists were likely to make short shrift of the Baptist plea for exemption. While the Privy Council was to disallow the law in 1771, this decision came only after the seizure and sale of Baptist lands and much public agitation.[51]

Joseph Hawley first entered this phase of the fight for religious freedom in 1770 when he served as chairman of a committee to consider a petition fron the Baptists at

[49] *Journal of Mass. House*, 1754, p. 186.
[50] Meyer, *op. cit.*, p. 50.
[51] *Ibid.*, pp. 54-67.

Ashfield and to investigate the entire matter of exemption for dissenters.[52] As a result a bill was brought in which shifted the burden to the towns by permitting them to exempt Baptists from religious taxes.[53] But the Baptists were not willing to allow the matter to rest here and continued their fight. In 1774, when the gulf between the Crown and the province of Massachusetts Bay was visibly widening, the problem of the dissenters cropped up again. Hawley was on a committee in February of that year to consider a petition from the Presbyterians for relief from supporting the Congregational ministry.[54] At the same session a bill was introduced and passed for the relief of both Quakers and Baptists, but because of the prorogation of the General Court it was never signed.[55]

In September of the following year, the Reverend Isaac Backus laid a Baptist memorial before the General Court.[56] It led to the introduction of a bill which Hawley strongly supported, arguing that the Baptists had been ill treated, that the establishment was not worth a groat and that he for one wished it might fall to the ground. But no agreement could be reached, and it was then proposed that the Baptists should withdraw their memorial. Hawley opposed this and said he hoped the memorial would lie in the files "till it had eaten out the present establishment."[57] So the fight for religious freedom rested temporarily; complete victory was still more than a half century away.

To return to the events of 1774 when the turning point had been reached, at least as far as Massachusetts was

[52] *Journal of Mass. House*, 1770, p. 93.
[53] *Ibid.*, 1770, pp. 141, 157, 169, 177.
[54] *Ibid.*, 1773, p. 128.
[55] *Ibid.*, 1773, pp. 185, 229, 237.
[56] A famous and contemporary account of the Baptist struggle is Isaac Backus' *History of New England with Particular Reference to the Baptists*.
[57] Dr. Asaph Fletcher to Isaac Backus. Oct. 31, 1775. In A. Hovey, *Life and Times of Issac Backus*, p. 227.

concerned. At Westminster legislation was enacted that was certain to arouse the fiercest opposition in the colonies, although of this the home government seemed sublimely unconscious. First in importance were the penalties for that colorful "tea-party" of the previous December. The port of Boston was closed to all commerce until restitution was made for the destruction of the property of the East India Company. Another act made it obligatory for local officials to provide barracks at the exact spot where troops were ordered. This was an amplification of the old Quartering Act, a direct response to the action of the Massachusetts General Court. Still another act modified the Massachusetts Charter. Councillors henceforth were to be appointed by the Crown instead of being elected by the house and council; in place of being elected by the freeholders, jurors were to be appointed by the sheriffs, and perhaps worst of all, the right of holding town meetings was to be greatly restricted.[58] The fourth, the Quebec Act, was an attempt to organize Canada and the West; its effects were disastrous although entirely unforeseen by Parliament. All the colonies interpreted the Quebec Act as an attack upon their liberties, while the attempt to enforce the Massachusetts Government Act brought about a complete breakdown in royal government in the province and a transfer of its functions to an essentially revolutionary, extra-legal organization.

The General Court, which Thomas Hutchinson had after all to face again, met on January 26 to listen to an innocuous message from the governor. Even reference to the recent tea-party was omitted. The house immediately returned to the old question of the payment of justices of the Superior Court, and it quickly became evident that this would be the feature of the session.[59] During the six months' recess of the legislature one of the justices had

[58] Channing, *op. cit.*, III, 152-53. See also William MacDonald, *Select Charters*, pp. 337-55.
[59] Hutchinson, *op. cit.*, III, 442.

been persuaded to accept the provincial salary instead of the grant from the Crown; before the convening of the General Court all but the chief justice had done likewise. When he definitely accepted the king's grant, conflict was inevitable. At the critical moment Hawley wrote home: "The Judges of the Superior Court all but the Chief Judge have accepted the Grants of the Province and have refused the King's grant and the Gen'l Court are about Petitioning for his removal"[60] Did Hawley, as he began to think of ousting the chief justice have any thought of his own treatment by that court not so long before? However, the principal problem was the means of removing the chief justice; such a proceeding was unprecedented and the house, while desirous to act, was loath to arouse the people to deeds of violence.

John Adams suggested impeachment. As the charter guaranteed all the rights and privileges of Englishmen and impeachment in Parliament was fairly common, the Massachusetts General Court might well follow its prototype. "Major Hawley," Adams says in his autobiography, "came to my house, and told me he heard I had broached a strange doctrine. He hardly knew what impeachment was; he had never read anyone, and never had thought on the subject. I told him he might read as many of them as he pleased, there stood the State Trials on the shelf, which was full of them, of all sorts, good and bad. I showed him Selden's works, in which there is a treatise on Judicature in Parliament, and gave it to him to read." Major Hawley talked the subject over with another friend, Judge Trowbridge, who had an extensive knowledge of the law. When talking with him Hawley "appealed to Lord Coke and Selden, as well as to the Charter, and advanced all the arguments which occurred to him. The Judge, although he had renounced the salary . . . was not much delighted with the subject on account of his brothers. He did, however, declare to the Major that he could not deny that the con-

[60] J. Hawley to Mercy Hawley, Jan. 10, 1774, Hawley Papers, I.

THE SONS OF LIBERTY    135

stitution had given the power to the House of Representatives . . . but that the exercise of it in this case would be vain, as the Council would undoubtedly acquit the Judge, even if they heard and tried the impeachment." Major Hawley, however, as one of the committee to prepare the resolves of impeachment only wanted to know the law. He proceeded with the work, bringing the articles to John Adams "to examine and discuss . . . paragraph by paragraph."[61]

While the resolves were under consideration, the superior court met at Boston. Peter Oliver, the chief justice, warned against attending, did not appear and the court adjourned. It never met again under royal auspices.[62] When the house resolves of impeachment were completed, Hawley was among those who presented them to the council and governor.[63] The council was ready to proceed with the impeachment but the governor refused to assume jurisdiction and to end the dispute he prorogued the session of the General Court until the seventh of June.[64]

During the interim Hawley, Samuel Adams, and the other radical leaders continued their work. As members of the committee of correspondence they sent on May 28 to the other colonies copies of the Boston Port Bill with their comments.[65] Hawley and Samuel Adams also were secretly approving resolutions for a Continental Congress and sending Massachusetts delegates to it.[66] The Port Bill went into effect on the first of June. The same day Thomas Hutchinson departed from his native land for England, leaving General Gage as governor of a province that was fast slipping from royal control.

As soon as the General Court convened, it began to select delegates to the Continental Congress. Samuel

[61] *Works of John Adams*, II, 330.
[62] Hutchinson, *op. cit.*, III, 444.
[63] *Journal of Mass. House*, 1773, p. 201.
[64] Hutchinson, *op. cit.*, III, 445.
[65] *Mass. Hist. Soc. Pro.*, Ser. I, XIII, 182.
[66] *Works of John Adams*, I, 144.

Adams, Robert Treat Paine, James Bowdoin and Joseph Hawley were chosen, but as Hawley, probably because of his chronic ill-health, declined to serve, John Adams took his place.[67] After the years of working together, the radical leaders from the Massachusetts coastal towns were to be separated from their steadfast supporter from Hampshire. General Gage, on hearing what was afoot in the Assembly, ordered its dissolution, but his secretary found the doors of the hall locked and had to be content with posting the notice of dissolution outside while the selection of delegates went on within.[68] Whether any one realized it or not, this was the real end of royal government in Massachusetts Bay.

Before long men were to see how momentous the events of the past few years had been, but at the time Gage's prorogation of the General Court on that June day seemed to be only one more incident in the constant quarrel between the governor and the legislature. Without much realization of what lay ahead, the Massachusetts delegates began to prepare for their trip to Philadelphia and attendance at the Continental Congress.

John Adams, for once a bit awed at the prospect before him and doubtful of his own capacities, wrote to Joseph Hawley for moral support and advice. The reply gave unreservedly of both. "I imagine," wrote the older man, "I have some knowledge of your abilities, and I assure you, Sir, I gave my vote for you most heartily, and I have not yet repented of it. My opinion is, that our committee, taken together, is the best we could have taken in the province." One of the soundest letters which Adams throughout his varied career ever received followed. Naturally much of Hawley's thought was on political matters, but on these, for fear that his letter might miscarry, he kept discreet silence. He only reminded Adams that "the people or State who will not or cannot defend

[67] *Ibid.*, I, 14.
[68] *Mass. State Papers*, p. 416.

their liberties and rights, will not have any for any long time. They will be slaves. Some other State will find it out, and will subjugate them."

Then Hawley turned to the matter of general conduct, expressing a breadth of view that is astonishing for a man who knew of little outside Massachusetts Bay. Coming from one provincial to another, it is surprising to read that the feelings of men representing different races, creeds, and colonies must be respected if the Congress were to be successful. Yet common sense might have shown even an Adams that a good deal of the success would depend on "the harmony, good understanding, and I had almost said brotherly love, of its members." Hawley realized that many of the colonies held the opinion "that the Massachusetts gentlemen, and especially of the town of Boston, do affect to dictate and take the lead in continental measures; ... are apt, from an inward vanity and self-conceit, to assume big and haughty airs." He was not certain how much foundation this had in fact, but was anxious "that everything in the conduct and behaviour of our gentlemen, which might tend to beget or strengthen such an opinion, might be carefully avoided." And, he continued: "It is highly probable, in my opinion, that you will meet gentlemen from several of the other colonies, fully equal to yourselves or any of you, in their knowledge of Great Britain, the colonies, law, history, government, commerce ... that it is very likely you may meet divers gentlemen in Congress, who are of Dutch or Scotch, or Irish extract. Many more there are in those southern colonies of those descents, than in these New England colonies, and many of them very learned and worthy men." To Hawley, then, prudence if nothing else seemed to advise "that everything should be very cautiously avoided which could give any least umbrage, disgust, or affront to any of such pedigree." As he saw clearly, "that which disparages our family, ancestors, or nation, is apt to stick by us if cast up in comparison, and their blood you will find as warm as ours."

In the end Joseph Hawley's devotion to political liberty would not down and he wrote with an emphasis which Adams could not mistake: "One thing I want the southern gentlemen should be deeply impressed with; that is, that all acts of British legislation which influence and affect our internal policy, are so absolutely repugnant to liberty and the idea of our being a free people, as taxation or revenue acts. Witness the present regulation act [the bill changing the Massachusetts Charter] for this province; and if we shall not be subdued by what is done already, like acts will undoubtedly be made for other colonies. I expect nothing but new treasons, new felonies, new misprisions, new praemunires, and not to say the Lord, the devil knows what."[69]

Hawley had hoped that the Massachusetts delegates would pass through Northampton on their way to Philadelphia and that he would have an opportunity to discuss the situation with them. But as they traveled by way of Springfield, he was compelled to forward his thoughts and ideas in writing, a "few broken hints" as he called them. His "broken hints," while containing some analysis of the position of the colonies, were at the same time as powerful a stimulant to revolution as the most ardent fire-eater could desire.

"We must fight," urged Hawley, "if we cannot otherwise rid ourselves of British taxation, all revenues, and the constitution or form of government enacted for us by the British parliament. It is evil against right ... It is *now* or never, that we must assert our liberty." The situation in Massachusetts troubled him especially and he questioned "whether the new government of this province shall be suffered to take place at all,—or whether it shall be immediately withstood and resisted ... I humbly conceive it not best, forcibly or wholly to resist it immediately.

[69] Hawley to John Adams, July 25, 1774. *Works of John Adams*, IX, 324.

There is not heat enough yet for battle," added the calculating revolutionist. "Constant, and a sort of negative resistance of government will increse the heat and blow the fire. There is not military skill enough. That is improving, and must be encouraged and improved. . . . Fight we must finally, unless Britain retreats." Here was a veritable clarion call to action!

But all should proceed cautiously. If fighting began before preparations were completed, before the colonies established a permanent union, "we shall be conquered, and all will be lost forever." Although Hawley was willing to go the limit if necessary, he suggested that, while the colonies were preparing to throw down the gage of battle, it might be well to negotiate with Great Britain. If the Mother Country should prove willing to "cede our rights and restore our liberties, all is well;" but on the other hand, if "she will not agree to relinquish and abolish all American revenues, under every pretence and name, all pretensions to order and regulate our internal policy and constitution —then . . . it will be time to take to arms."

The man who had favored the Albany Plan of Union twenty years before was not likely now to lose sight of the need for colonial union.[70] "Our salvation depends upon our established persevering union of the colonies," he wrote. "All possible devices and endeavors must be used to establish, improve, brighten and maintain such union . . . is it not absolutely necessary that some plan be settled for a continuation of Congress?" Realist that he was, he saw where this action would lead, and hastened to add: "We must be aware that congresses will be declared and enacted by parliament to be high treason."[71]

[70] *Journal of Mass. House*, 1754. p. 182.

[71] *Works of John Adams*, IX, app. It is also to be found in Hezekiah Niles' *Principles and Acts of the Revolution*, pp. 324-25. When Adams was sending the original "broken hints" to Niles in 1819, he wrote: "I pray you send it back to me. I would not exchange this original for the show book of Harvard College."

In the fall of 1774 Hawley's words were too strong for most men; how great was their influence when circulated in the Continental Congress can never be known. To one man, at least, they were as milk and honey. John Adams said many years later that when he showed the "broken hints" to Patrick Henry, the Virginian burst out: "By God, I am of that man's mind!"[72]

[72] This outburst of Henry's is recorded in a letter from John Adams to William Wirt written Jan. 23, 1818. *Works of John Adams*, X, 277.

## Chapter VIII
## A LEADER OF MASSACHUSETTS

When General Gage dissolved the Massachusetts Assembly in June, 1774, he did not dream that he was terminating royal government in the province. Probably the time had long passed when actual revolution could have been averted; certainly no effective compromise was possible after the governor's secretary posted the fatal notice of dissolution. A creeping paralysis afflicted royal government after that June day. Juries refused to appear and act while Chief Justice Oliver remained in office; as a result the courts became dormant. In August the names of the mandamus councillors were announced, but a hostile public opinion forced most of them to resign their appointments. Royal officials, harassed and intimidated, failed to carry on their functions and real power passed to the local committees of correspondence which were being organized in every town. Meanwhile, the Massachusetts Government Act which had so ruthlessly altered the traditional political system of the province remained ineffective.[1]

At Northampton there was sharp division of sentiment. Joseph Hawley was, of course, the leader of the radicals, but his cousins the Stoddards were staunch loyalists. Even his dear pastor, John Hooker, who had married John Worthington's sister, was uncertain what position to take. Worthington, that lifelong colleague at the bar, could never forget that he had been the king's servant; he was about to forsake position and power as a sacrifice

[1] H. A. Cushing, *Transition from Provincial to Commonwealth Government in Massachusetts*, Ch. iii, *passim*.

to a loyalist conscience. The Williamses and Colonel Oliver Partridge at Hatfield were notorious partisans of the king, and while they had long been political opponents of Hawley and his friends, their social and economic interterests were not far apart. Hawley had moved a long way in the preceding decade; perhaps without too much thought of the consequences, he had come to be allied inextricably with the radical side. Family and social position should have made of him a Tory; but accident, possibly the old dislike of Israel Williams, together with some careful reasoning and a due amount of rationalization, placed him among the Patriots.

By late summer Hampshire County had been drawn into the current of unrest. On August 26, a convention met at Hadley to "consult about the courts going on." Although there was still a deal of moderate sentiment, before the week was out the Court of General Sessions at Springfield had been broken up by a well-behaved mob, marching with "staves & musick." John Worthington at the same time was forced to renounce his appointment as a mandamus councillor, but even this did not save his house from being invaded.[2]

Soon afterward, on September 13, Northampton chose its first committee of correspondence; Joseph Hawley was the chairman.[3] Ten days later some of the members of the committee were representing the town at a county convention which had been called to deliberate on measures suitable to "this time of publick calamity and distress."[4] The convention affirmed its allegiance to George III but did not hesitate to suspend the acts of his Parliament in so far as they affected Hampshire County and to resolve that the provincial taxes should be withheld from the province treasurer, Harrison Gray. As a practical point, the convention advised the people of the county to use "the

[2] Trumbull, *op. cit.*, II, 345-48.
[3] Northampton Town Records, Sept. 13, 1774.
[4] *Ibid.*, Sept. 19, 1774. Mass. Hist. Soc.

# A LEADER OF MASSACHUSETTS 143

utmost diligence, forthwith, to acquaint themselves with the military art, under the command and direction of such persons as they shall choose, and that they furnish themselves with the full lawfull quantity of ammunition, and good, effective arms, as soon as may be, for that purpose." It is not difficult to see behind this advice the influence of the author of "a few broken hints." The delegates also heartily approved the selection of representatives to a provincial congress which would take the place of the new General Court which Gage expected to convene at Salem in October.[5] But soon after the meeting of the Hampshire convention, the governor cancelled the writs of election, a futile gesture because by that time his real power had vanished.

Before the meeting of the county convention, Hawley persuaded a majority of the Northampton selectmen to sign a warrant for a town meeting to elect delegates to a provincial congress.[6] At this meeting on September 29, Joseph Hawley and Seth Pomeroy were chosen to represent the town at the First Provincial Congress.[7] Then these "true and loyal subjects of George the third" voted approval of the resolutions of the recent county convention.

Already the problem of restoring stable government was troubling the radical leaders as well as the royal supporters. Hawley had declared himself in favor of resuming the old charter, and in spite of his caution had said that if the four New England governments would support such a meaure, he would "venture his life to carry and defend it against the whole force of Great Britain."[8] The Provincial Congress which convened at Salem on October 7, 1774, although fundamentally an extra-legal body, was the first step towards stability under a new order. After

[5] Trumbull, *op. cit.*, II, 349.
[6] Northampton Town Records, Sept. 26, 1774. Mass. Hist. Society.
[7] Trumbull, *op. cit.*, II, 351-52.
[8] Thomas Young to S. Adams, Sept. 4, 1774. S. Adams Papers, New York Public Library.

its organization even the most obtuse Tory could not doubt that Massachusetts Bay was in revolt.

Joseph Hawley was the leader in this congress, and for two years he was to be one of the principal leaders of Massachusetts. The two Adamses were at Philadelphia now and their mantles fell naturally to the "river god." He sat on all the important committees, those to take into consideration the state of the province, to consider measures for defense and the committee of safety which acted as the executive when the congress was not in session.[9] On these committees he was associated with many men whose public careers were just beginning: John Hancock, Elbridge Gerry and his good friend James Sullivan, for instance, all of whom were to become governors of the state and one a vice-president of the still undreamed of federal union. Hawley's work on the committee to consider the state of the province was concerned with finance, the life-blood of any movement, and it was he who recommended the payment of taxes to a receiver-general set up by the congress rather than the legal province treasurer, Harrison Gray.[10] This concern with finance was only a continuation of his old familiarity with revenue measures and appropriations. The interference with tax collection was open revolt, and at least temporarily it gave the revolutionary government some economic strength. When the Massachusetts leaders began to look longingly towards Canada, Hawley served on the committee which corresponded with Quebec and Montreal in the beginning of the vain struggle for a "fourteenth colony." Behind the scenes the all-important tasks of organization were continued. Outwardly the work of the congress was colorless but its very formation and meeting were revolutionary steps; the next move waited on the action of the royal power.

Hawley all the while was keeping his eyes and ears open. He suspected Charles Lee, that soldier of fortune, con-

[9] *Journal of Each Provincial Congress*, pp. 16, 23, 36.
[10] *Ibid.*, p. 38.

sidering him "about as Subtil a tool as any of the friends of Government"—one to beware of. To Samuel Adams he wrote that Lord Percy, who within a few months was to gain a dubious reputation, says "he is *well* with the selectmen of Boston. Sometimes men in such Stations really affect to gain and have a high pleasure in the esteem and affections of the people and if by sounding him you should find it to be really his turn, perhaps by Cultivating that temper, without putting too great confidence in him, his Friendship may be Secured and perhaps some jealousies may arise between him and Genl. Gage and thereby the plans of Administration clogged. I know you will improve every advantage which may turn up."[11] The friends were not above a little plotting and intriguing if it might chance to aid the colonial side.

When the Second Provincial Congress convened at Cambridge at the beginning of February, Hawley threw himself into the multitudinous concerns of state. He was associated particularly with military problems, perhaps from his experience in the French and Indian wars or because all men of standing were credited with military ability, but more probably from his good sense and the general confidence which the public reposed in him. Long experience in public life was mellowing him, and the changed status of the province gave him a feeling of responsibility that had not been so marked in earlier years. Besides, he had passed the half century mark now, and middle-aged men are seldom the leaders of violent revolution. The tone of his "broken hints" gave place to moderation and caution. He had no thought of turning back; one must press onward, but only slowly; there must be no reckless rushing over precipices in the dark—such was the tenor of his constant correspondence with Samuel Adams, Thomas Cushing and Elbridge Gerry. Such was the tone of letters, but close at hand was the real situation; the old

[11] Hawley to S. Adams, Dec. 16, 1774. S. Adams Papers.

royal province was in revolt against constituted authority, and Hawley, unlike so many of his colleagues, was never blind as to where this would lead. So the problem of defense took his time and abilities up to and beyond the limit of his strength.

During this first month of the second congress he was on the leading committees as before. With others he expressed in a resolution the determination of the people to support their rights "cooly and resolutely" and "at all hazards." Shortly before the congress adjourned he with his old friends, Samuel Adams, Gerry and Cushing, pointed out, in another resolve to the people, the perils of their situation because the British ministry and Parliament seemed ready to destroy the people of Massachusetts Bay.[12]

When Hawley returned home in late February he was "very low and melancholy." The old ailment was returning again, and he could think of nothing but the difficulties of the province, how the towns were not paying their taxes, the great lack of gunpowder, and the unmistakable trend toward hostilities with the Mother Country.[13] Furthermore, an outburst of violence in Hampshire County disturbed his sense of order. Early in February his relatives at Hatfield, doughty old Israel Williams and his son, had been seized by a mob, carried across the river to Hadley, and given a mock trial. After being shut in a smoke-filled house, they had been forced to sign a confession of opposition to the Whig cause. A day later, a mob from Pelham came to inflict similar treatment upon another cousin, Major Solomon Stoddard, to whom most of the members were in debt.[14] Society seemed chaotic. Worn out physically and mentally, Hawley was inactive in public life for nearly two months because of his "want of health or memory, weakness of body and Shocking impair of mind."[15]

[12] *Journal of Each Prov. Congress*, p. 101.
[13] Hawley to Theodore Sedgwick, May 10, 1775. Hawley Papers, II.
[14] Judd Manuscript. Revolutionary Matters, p. 169.
[15] Hawley to Sedgwick, May 10, 1775. Hawley Papers, II.

Before these clouds had enveloped him entirely he wrote a long letter to Thomas Cushing, his old associate who had for years been speaker of the house of representatives, at Boston urging a policy of moderation and care. Especially was he concerned lest the minute men should be mustered too quickly by the provincial committee of safety. As he pointed out, whenever the minute men should be called out, they would naturally suppose it their duty to fight, and would seek only how to fight to the best advantage. These men would not stop to consider whether the time was ripe, nor what effect their plunging into hostilities would have on other colonies. The committee of safety must move slowly, because as Hawley saw clearly, hostilities once begun "will, thenceforward continue, and be vigorously pushed, until the fate of America be decided."

But without the support of the other colonies Massachusetts would certainly be overwhelmed. Hawley did not consider the "Declaration of Rights" and the "Association" drawn up by the Continental Congress in October, 1774, as a sufficient guarantee of support. Donations such as had been given to the poor of Boston would be a poor kind of support. By every means possible, hostilities must be avoided until the other colonies had given an "express, categorical decision" that the hour is struck and that they would support Massachusetts to the utmost. "When once the blow is struck," he urged, "it must be followed, and we must conquer, or all is lost forever. If we are not supported, perseveringly supported, by divers other Colonies, can we expect anything else than in a short time to fall a prey to our enemies? May God make us consider it." As a final word of warning, Hawley pointed out that under Gage's protection a superior court was sitting at Boston—and that might well be dangerous. "If they get a grand jury," he wrote, "then they probably will obtain indictments of high treason; and indictments will not be procured without a view and respect to arrests and commitments, convictions, hangings, drawings and quarterings. What your chance will be I need not tell you."[16]

When Cushing replied a few days later he agreed entirely with Major Hawley's sentiments. In words which were almost an echo, he accepted the ideas put forth by Hawley and promised to communicate the absent member's memorandum to the committee of safety. For his own part he would urge the principle that "nothing but an absolute necessity of preserving ourselves from immediate and sudden destruction can satisfy us with other Colonies in commencing Hostilities."[17]

Before long, however, the minute men did muster to preserve Massachusetts from "immediate and sudden destruction," and the Lord Percy who had been so "well with the selectmen of Boston" rescued only with difficulty his fellow soldiers from the torments of the swarms from "every Middlesex village and farm." At Northampton Joseph Hawley was still sunk in despondency and because of his continued absence from the Provincial Congress people were beginning to whisper that he was no longer loyal to the popular cause. In February he had expressed very strong disapproval of the Whig outrages on the Tories, and he had been seeing a good deal of those out-and-out Tories, the Stoddards. It was rumored too, that he had been reading Tory literature; one could not be sure. Finally Theodore Sedgwick could stand the uncertainty no longer and wrote to Hawley for an explanation.

The reply must have laid all suspicions. Hawley's spirits were recovering and he wrote with all his oldtime forcefulness. He admitted very frankly that Major Stoddard had called and had brought him some pamphlets. These Hawley had fully intended to read, because, as he wrote Sedgwick, "I told [Stoddard] I was entirely open to conviction, that I endeavored to hear and see all that was said and wrote on both sides." But as it happened, Hawley

[16] Hawley to Cushing, Feb. 22, 1775. Mass. Archives, CXCIII, 33.
[17] Cushing to Hawley. Feb. 27, 1775. Hawley Papers, II.

was too ill to read and before he had recovered sufficiently to do so, Stoddard sent for the pamphlets. His loyalty to the cause, however, was undiminished and he must have expelled any remaining doubts in Sedgwick's mind when he wrote: "My life my estate my all in the world is aboard the same bark with my country's cause and I wish I was able to do more to Save them all. But my opinion is that right and liberty will be maintained in this land whether I shall be able to contribute any more to it or not."[18]

Toward the end of May, 1775 Hawley was so far recovered that he could return to the congress at Cambridge and, although he was never to be wholly well again, he threw himself with even greater vigor into the work of government. With others he considered the effectual and ready organization of the Massachusetts army, particularly the exasperating plague of too many officers, for every man wanted to command.[19] To him regularly fell the perplexing questions which arose from Ethan Allen's capture of Ticonderoga on Lake Champlain and which were accompanied by the problem of complicated intercolonial relationships.

Benedict Arnold had been commissioned more or less secretly by the Massachusetts Committee of Safety to raise 400 men in the western part of the province for the capture of the fort. Possibly the committee was moved principally by the thought of the valuable military stores at Ticonderoga; in any case that was the explanation sent to the New York authorities to excuse the trespassing of Arnold and his men on New York territory. But when Arnold arrived in western Massachusetts, he found that other plans were afoot. Ethan Allen, an embattled farmer residing in what is now Vermont but was then territory in dispute between New Hampshire and New York, was raising with the more or less clandestine support of Connecticut another expedition. Arnold's position was legally

---

[18] Hawley to Sedgwick, May 11, 1775. Hawley Papers, II.
[19] *Journal of Each Prov. Congress*, p. 246.

the stronger, but he tactfully recognized local sentiments and accepted joint command with Allen.[20]

The success of the attack upon Ticonderoga necessitated considerable explanation and investigation, particularly in the soothing of the ever-touchy inter-colonial nerves. Much of this work was Hawley's. As chairman of a somewhat mystified committee of the congress he wrote to the Massachusetts commissioners at the fort for "copies of the Commission and every Paper containing the appointment of Col. Benedict Arnold to a Secret Warlike enterprise to the Westward, of the instructions given him... of engagements to him in behalf of this colony if any Such authority was given him, his orders respecting the ordinance at Ticonderoga and places on Lake Champlain and every thing necessary to give the congress a full understanding of the relation, Col. Arnold has Stood and now stands in to this Colony."[21] Hoping to calm any ill-feeling that might have arisen from Arnold's work, Hawley wrote officially to the Provincial Congress of New York. He urged the New Yorkers to seize all arms or ammunition belonging to the Crown while declaring that the cannon which were being brought from Ticonderoga to Massachusetts were to be considered as the property of all the colonies.[22] A similar letter was sent to the governor of Connecticut with the further advice that the fortresses on Lake Champlain should be held at all costs.[23] This idea of guarding the all-important route to Canada was one to which Hawley returned frequently. When the congress at Cambridge sent delegates to examine conditions at Ticonderoga their instructions were prepared by a committee under Hawley's chairmanship.[24]

[20] This entire episode is set forth in J. H. Smith, *Our Struggle for the Fourteenth Colony*, Vol. I, ch. iv. See also John Pell, *Ethan Allen*.

[21] Hawley to Capt. Jonathan Brown, May 26, 1775. Mass. Archives, CXCIII, 249.

[22] *Journal of Each Prov. Congress*, p. 258.

[23] *Ibid.*, p. 266.

[24] *Ibid.*, p. 321.

## A LEADER OF MASSACHUSETTS 151

Ticonderoga was only one problem. Business crowded in rapidly and Hawley, now vice-president of the Congress, shifted from one field of activity to another. One day he was at work on an address to the Continental Congress seeking advice on a settled government for Massachusetts; on another, he had to consider a resolve for the increase of arms.[25] The army, still a province affair, had been raised by popular leaders who as a reward expected commissions; from this a knotty problem developed which Hawley and his committee failed to unravel.[26] The events of Bunker Hill on the seventeenth of June renewed the energies of those concerned with military matters, and after dispatching an account of the battle to the Congress at Philadelphia, Hawley and his fellows turned to the disposition of troops.[27] Companies were drawn into Cambridge from the outlying towns; the lack of discipline was considered, although ineffectually; and then began the flurry of preparation for the reception of the newly appointed commander-in-chief, General George Washington of Virginia. Joseph Hawley with two others was chosen to meet Washington at Springfield, but Hawley, far too important to leave Cambridge on ceremonial missions, was excused and stayed in Cambridge, where he was working with the committees which were preparing an address to Washington and were seeking a suitable residence for the general.[28] Of far more importance were the letters which were prepared under Hawley's direction to solicit aid from Connecticut and the Continental Congress in the collection of the greatly-needed and indispensable powder.

Meanwhile, the heat of the New England summer was making the members of this third and last Provincial Congress anxious to bring their labors to a conclusion. As the session ended, the committee of safety which was still

[25] *Ibid.*, p. 319, 340.
[26] *Ibid.*, p. 325.
[27] *Ibid.*, p. 353.
[28] *Ibid.*, p. 391, 400, 418.

under Hawley's direction, harassed and overworked, turned from one problem to another and finally to finance. More experienced men in later times, men who considered themselves mature in matters of finance, have taken the same fatal step in financial policy now taken by the Massachusetts Committee of Safety—the emission of paper money.[29] It would haunt them all for many a day.

At the Continental Congress that summer plans were afoot for a conference between the Indians of the Six Nations and the Commissioners of Indian Affairs for the Northern Department. Hawley was elected one of the five commissioners with General Philip Schuyler, Volkert P. Dorn of Albany, Oliver Wolcott of Connecticut and Turbot Francis of Philadelphia. Thomas Cushing writing to Hawley about this selection, said: "I thought you well qualified for this important trust and accordingly with the rest of my brethren I recommended you to the Congress. I hope it will be agreeable to you to attend to this appointment. All my fear is least the critical and perplexed situation of our Province should require your constant attendance at the General Court."[30] But Hawley's health as well as the demands of the province would not permit his acceptance of the post. He was forced to send a refusal to the Congress, at the same time expressing the assurance that if his health were less precarious, no service that he could think of would be more agreeable.[31]

Massachusetts, following the advice of the Continental Congress, now resumed its old charter, adapting it where necessary to the changed conditions. Thus Hawley's constant hope for a return to stable government had been fulfilled. The governor was gone and in his place the council acted as the executive, but otherwise there was little change. Hawley was back at his old seat as representative for

[29] *Ibid.*, p. 424.
[30] Cushing to Hawley, July 24, 1775. Burnett, *Letters of Members of Congress*, I, 176.
[31] *Journal of Continental Congress*, II, 247n.

## A LEADER OF MASSACHUSETTS

Northampton and once more he was busy with the multitudinous affairs before the General Court. Financial or military matters, the design for a province seal, the procuring of munitions or the manufacture of saltpetre, all seemed to lie within his powers. John Adams had recommended him to Washington as a man of judgment and integrity; perhaps because of this Hawley was in close and frequent contact with the general.[32] On several occasions he attempted the impossible in trying to explain the idiosyncrasies of Massachusetts military organization.[33] At Washington's first suspicion of Dr. Church's treason Hawley and James Warren were called in.[34] And it was Hawley who was often sent on official committees to discuss with Washington conditions at Machias, the Massachusetts troops in the Continental Army, or the need for medical supplies.[35]

Periodically Hawley was at home where town and county affairs, as always, demanded his attention. He was the moderator of the town meetings, even as in calmer days, and was still the first selectman. Prisoners of war were billeted at Northampton and the problem of feeding, clothing and sheltering them came to his already busy hands.[36] The Provincial Congress had placed him on a committee to receive the reports from Hampshire County committees of correspondence. Because he was the best known man on the committee most of the reports were addressed to him; throughout the summer of 1775 he was receiving assurances from the Hampshire villages that they were loyal to the cause of liberty and to the various resolves of the Provincial and Continental Congresses.[37] The committees of safety in the county in these and succeeding months held numerous

[32] *Writings of John Adams, op. cit.*, IX, 359.
[33] Hawley to S. Adams, Nov. 12, 1775. S. Adams Papers.
[34] *Warren-Adams Letters*, I, 122 *Mass. Hist. Soc. Coll.*
[35] *Journal of Mass. House*, 1775. I, 61, 116; II, 72.
[36] *Mass. Acts and Resolves*, XXX, 118, 144; *Journal of Mass. House*, 1775, I, 253.
[37] There are many of these reports in the Hawley Papers, II.

conventions. At them all Hawley was the leading figure and in this manner he became the mainspring of the revolutionary movement in western Massachusetts.[38]

Somwhere, also, the details of private life must have been present, however deeply submerged. Hawley's farm land had long since been rented to others; for years he had kept practically no livestock. His law practice, of course, had almost disappeared with the closing of the courts. Now family affairs rested with the competent Mercy who saw that the household ran as smoothly as ever and provided an occasional refuge for her famous husband whom Samuel Adams described at this time as possessing the stern virtue and spirit of a Roman Censor.[39]

When the second session of the revived General Court ended early in November, 1775, Hawley sent a review of its chief activities to Samuel Adams at Philadelphia. Its principal difficulty had been concerned with that hardy perennial, the appointment of officers. Because of certain contradictory resolves of the Continental Congress, the house insisted on exercising this power in common with the executive board or council. Even in a time of crisis the house was over-jealous of its rights. Hawley, cautious as ever, suggested to Adams that the Continental Congress might well ignore the entire dispute, particularly as an unpopular decision could "ruin this colony and Shock the continent." The Royal Proclamation of Rebellion which had been issued on August 23 Hawley called the "clumsy Ministerial declaration of war" and as a result, he said, "the eyes of all the continent are fastened on your body to see whether you on this occasion act with firmness and intrepidity and with the Spirit and dispatch which our situation calls for, if you should do so we are safe, if otherwise our state may be hazardous. It is time to know who are friends and who are foes and to be effectively on our guard against the latter."

[38] G. Sheldon, *History of Deerfield*, II, 721.
[39] *Writings of S. Adams*, III, 238.

Hawley had no sympathy with or tolerance for the sea coast towns which sold provisions to British vessels, because he felt certain that if the vessels could not obtain supplies, they would soon be unable to keep the sea. Better sacrifice a few towns if necessary—experience had shown that supplying enemy ships was no protection from destruction. In his mind, Falmouth (Portland) for example, which had recently been burned deserved no pity. "They made no provisions for their defence, did not improve that which the government made for them, and have experienced that destruction which their temporizing deceit and poltroonery deserved."[40] These were the words of a harsh realist, but he was not speaking for public consumption.

At about the same time Hawley wrote to John Adams, who was also at Philadelphia, urging a Congressional bounty to encourage the enlistment of privates. But Adams was forced to reply that Congress was cold to the proposition and would allow only forty shillings a month as salary, because, as he pointed out, local prejudice, opinions and principles stood in the way and could not be changed overnight.

The characters of gentlemen in the four New England colonies differ as much from those in the others, as that of the common people differs; that is as much as several distinct nations almost. Gentlemen, men of sense or any kind of education, in the other colonies, are much fewer in proportion than in New England. ... I dread the consequences of this dissimilitude of character, and without the utmost caution on both sides, and the most considerate forbearance with one another and prudent condescension on both sides, they will certainly be fatal. The winter will cast the die. For God's sake, therefore, reconcile our people to what has been done, for you may depend upon it that nothing more can be done here, and I should shudder at the thought of proposing a bounty.[41]

Possibly Adams would have done well to reread Hawley's year-old letter of advice, although his account of the situation was probably only too true.

[40] Hawley to S. Adams, Nov. 12, 1775. S. Adams Papers.
[41] J. Adams to Hawley, Nov. 25, 1775. Burnet, *op. cit.*, I, 259.

## A LEADER OF MASSACHUSETTS

Hawley, unlike so many Sons of Liberty, had long foreseen independence and understood that events were tending steadily in that direction. Others might rationalize the colonial position, might attempt to sidestep cold logic, but not he, and as the early months of 1776 passed he talked and wrote for independence. His constant agitation for a declaration of independence and his steady attention to military problems were his work that year.

These were the days of Hawley's maturity; the mellowing was completed. On his frequent trips across Massachusetts he was regarded with interest and respect. When the word arrived at a tavern, Howe's at Marlboro or Colonel Williams' on the Bay Path, that Major Hawley was coming, all would be astir. While someone rushed forth to hold his horse, another poked up the fire; the landlord made ready to receive him and the small boy would be sent running through town to inform leading citizens that Major Hawley had come. And while he rested before the fire or sipped his toddy, important men came to talk with one who had become far more than a "river god."[42]

In February, *Common Sense* fell into Hawley's hands and he read it with avidity, writing to Elbridge Gerry that "every sentiment has sunk into my well-prepared heart" which was "like good ground well prepared for good seed." He had long been thinking of the need for a supreme government based on a wisely designed constitution, but had seen it only as a corollary to independence. Without independence such a government would be impossible and without such a government the colonies would be but a rope of sand, unable to maintain themselves. If for no other reason, he wrote Gerry, a well-established, independent government was necessary to solve the problem of the rising floods

[42] William Bolter who lived in the Hawley household for some years made a trip across Massachusetts with Hawley at about this time. Although only a boy the experience made a great impression on him. His reminiscences are recorded in the Judd Manuscript, I, 477.

of paper currency.⁴³ But in Massachusetts, at least, Hawley had been one of those who had let loose this flood.

He saw clearly the need for commerce with foreign nations to maintain defense, but this could be obtained only by an independent state which could give merchants the privilege of trading with all nations of the world. Such a government, in a world still dominated by mercantilist theory, would rally to its support all those interested in business and trade. Besides, the non-importation and non-consumption agreements were of no value; they had never been kept and were only an irresistible temptation to trade, both for profits and subsistence. Hawley was realist enough to admit that. "Independence," he insisted, "is the only way to union and harmony, to vigour and dispatch in business; our eye will be single, and our whole body full of light; anything short of it will, as appears to me, be our destruction, infallible destruction, and that speedily. Amen."⁴⁴

When Boston was evacuated in March he refused to join in the general rejoicing; his celebration was reserved until Congress should declare independence.⁴⁵ As he wrote to Samuel Adams, until the United Colonies were as independent of Great Britain as any state which enters into treaties with her, "united" was but a word of sound without meaning. Consistency, or common sense if you like, made independence the only conclusion to all the months of repelling force with force, of appointing officers and securing ammunition, even of non-importation. Massachusetts had not worked alone; ever since Lexington she had had the active support of Congress and apparently of the other colonies. This support indicated that the colonies together were strong enough to maintain their position. But again

---

⁴³ Hawley to Gerry, Feb. 18, 1776. P. Force *American Archives*, 4th Ser., Vol. 4, p. 1190.

⁴⁴ Hawley to Gerry, Feb. 20, 1776. Force, *op. cit.*, 4th Ser., Vol. 4, p. 1220.

⁴⁵ *Warren-Adams Letters*, I, 224.

with independence must come confederation to preserve it and to insure unity. Popular sentiment, Hawley assured Adams, was moving rapidly towards independence and Congress must be wary lest it lag behind public opinion. Otherwise ruin might well ensue. It was within the realm of possibility, he added, for "the army or great Mobb made up partly of your own army and partly of others to drive down on you and disperse you and appoint others from among themselves to take your place and dictate for the whole continent.... The People are now ahead of you and the only way to prevent discord and indescretion is to strike while the iron is hot. The People's blood is so hot as not to admit of delays.... For God's Sake make the best ... Constitution you can and give it out or the Lord only knows who we Shall have for our leaders. It is now or never."[46]

Samuel Adams who had advocated or at least hoped for independence in the days when the cause was only a controversy, hastened to place himself in whole-hearted agreement with Hawley. He could see no reason against a definite declaration of independence. After raising an army and navy, arming privateers against British shipping, and violating all the regulations of trade, Americans could hardly consider themselves or expect others to consider them other than as independent. Yet Adams who for the moment was without his customary rashness added: "But let us not be impatient. It requires Time to convince the doubting and inspire the timid."[47]

Hawley's bombardment of the Massachusetts delegates with his version of "Carthago delenda est" continued as a cold, windy April gave way to the mildness of May. To Gerry he insisted that independence was necessary to make the Tory position definitely treasonable and he reiterated the connection between independence and an abiding union.

[46] Hawley to S. Adams, April 1, 1776. S. Adams Papers.
[47] S. Adams to Hawley, April 15, 1776. *Writings of S. Adams, op. cit.*, III, 277.

## A LEADER OF MASSACHUSETTS

Without it taxation was not feasible nor trade prosperous, and most of all—that old love of Hawley's—union with Canada could not be achieved. "Without a real Continental government," he continued, "an Army will overrun us, and people will by and by, sooner than you may be aware of, call for their old Constitution, and as they did in England after Cromwell's death, call in Charles the Second. For *God's* sake let there be a full revolution or all had been done in vain. Independency and a well planned Continental Government will save us."[48] Nor did he allow Samuel Adams to forget that in Massachusetts people were ripe for a complete breaking away from Britain. Without this he foresaw civil war, because at least two-thirds of the people were for independence and would accept nothing less, even if it meant fighting with Congress should that body prove over-conservative. "If the united Colonies," he "do not become an independent People or one united common Wealth they will cease to be a people.... A resolution for independence unites the whole and will be universally Submitted to perhaps with reluctancy by some. But I believe with more general consent than was any government in England or Great Britain."[49]

Hawley, more and more concerned with the problems arising from paper currency, saw here an additional argument for independence. Notes of all the colonies as well as the Continental bills were circulating in Massachusetts to the derangement of economic life. It was worse than in the old royal days when he had tried to exclude the bills of other colonies from the Bay. The economic situation gave the Tories a workable criticism of the colonial cause that might in the end prove most effective. It seemed to Hawley that an improvement might follow the setting up of a confederation which would regulate currency.[50] His

[48] Hawley to Gerry, May 1, 1776. Force, *op. cit.*, 4th Ser., Vol. 5, p. 1168.
[49] Hawley to S. Adams, May 17, 1776. S. Adams Papers.
[50] Hawley to Gerry, June 2-6, 1776. S. Adams Papers.

ardent zeal for the cause in which both he and Gerry were so deep never flagged. By mid-June about two-thirds of the Massachusetts towns had voted for independence and more were falling into line. They further strengthened Hawley's stand and his reiterated contention that the province was ripe for independence. He wrote to Gerry: "You cannot declare Independence too soon; but the Confederation must be formed with great deliberation."[51]

He had not long to wait now and on the fifth of July Gerry sent copies of the Declaration of Independence to General Warren; one of these was intended for his indefatigable correspondent. A few days later Samuel Adams wrote to Hawley: "The Congress has at length declared the Colonies free and independent States. Upon this I congratulate you, for I know your heart has long been set upon it."[52] The first line had been won; whether the position could be maintained or not would be the next question.

Meanwhile Hawley had been actively engaged in the ramifications of New England defense—general strategy, the raising and equipping of troops, and the manufacture of gunpowder. Between times he aided in the transition from province to commonwealth government. Details such as altering the style of writs, processes and other legal procedures fell to him. He reported bills for the disposal of Tory and refugee estates.[53] In committee he considered orders and regulations for the militia, and when the army was temporarily overstocked with blankets, he reported a resolve stopping further collection.[54] He conferred with Washington on raising a regiment to reinforce the army in Canada, and then had to contrive ways to encourage the

[51] Hawley to Gerry, June 13, 1776. Force, *op. cit.*, 4th Ser., Vol. 6, p. 866.
[52] S. Adams to Hawley, July 9, 1776, *Writings of S. Adams, op. cit.*, III, 294.
[53] *Journal of Mass. House*, 1775, II, 119; III, 19.
[54] *Ibid.*, 1775, II, 105, 167.

## A LEADER OF MASSACHUSETTS

building of powder mills.[55] When the House adjourned in February, Hawley went home as an agent in Hampshire County to collect gold and silver in exchange for Continental bills, for the army in Canada badly needed hard money.[56] One had to be versatile to keep up in the race.

One of the early plans of the revolutionary leaders was for the invasion of Canada in the hope that the thirteen United Colonies might become fourteen.[57] This idea was not entirely an early expression of American expansionist sentiment but was inspired by the fear of a Canada under British control and also by apprehensions lest the Quebec Act of 1774 should set up institutions which would be hostile to those of the rest of the colonies. In any case, by the autumn of 1775 two expeditions were on their way towards Quebec. One under Richard Montgomery was following the traditional Lake Champlain route; the other led by Benedict Arnold was toiling up the Kennebec and through the forests of Maine. Although Montgomery was able to take Montreal, an assault on Quebec by the combined American forces at the end of 1775 was a disastrous failure.

Canada had always interested Hawley, and with Washington he believed that the salvation of the country depended on the success of the Arnold-Montgomery expedition.[58] Before any definite news came in he wrote to Samuel Adams: "We trust that your Congress don't starve that expedition, if we Succeed in that territory Great Britain will be Shocked. You will see that our enemies regret their neglect upon Hudson's river, our future Safety very much depends upon our vigilance and Sweep in that quarter May heaven direct you."[59]

[55] *Ibid.*, 1775, II, 167, 281.
[56] *Mass Acts & Resolves*, XIX, 266.
[57] The classic account of the attempt to conquer Canada is Justin H. Smith's *Our Struggle for the Fourteenth Colony*, 2 vols.
[58] See C. H. Van Tyne, *War of Independence: American Phase*, p. 79, for some discussion of this subject.
[59] Hawley to S. Adams, Nov. 12, 1775. S. Adams Papers.

Throughout the strenuous months Canada was always in his mind, and he urged Gerry, when the latter was setting out for Philadelphia early in 1776, to do his utmost that enough first-class troops should be marched to Canada and that adequate provision should be made for their pay, clothing, food and arms.[60] To Samuel Adams, also, he talked of Canada, particularly in its relation to possible British control of the Hudson. The possibility of free communication between the British and the Indians, Dutch and Scotch he felt to be full of danger, although the Dutch and Scotch were less to be feared than the Tories everywhere. So strongly did he feel this, that he wrote: "I shall scarce ever fail in any of my letters to any of our Worthy Delegates of stirring up their pure minds by way of remembrance touching New York and the whole North River, the city of Quebeck and the river St. Lawrence above it."[61] Adams replied that he was certain the original British plan had been to conquer New England by divorcing it from the other colonies through British control of the Hudson; this plan he insisted had never been given up. An attack on New York might be expected; failure there would most likely be followed by return to Boston.[62] Actually, of course, Adams was only guessing about British strategy; both he and Hawley were recalling the French and Indian wars when they talked of Canada or the Hudson.

When dispatches in the spring of 1776 announced the final rout of the decimated army before Quebec, Hawley was beside himself. In haste and great agitation he wrote Samuel Adams: "For God's and the land's Sake Sustain augment Support your army in Canada. Call for Carriages, Bread and Meat in New England. We are in fears there

[60] Hawley to Gerry, Feb. 18, 1775. Force, *op. cit.*, 4th Ser., Vol. 4, p. 1190.

[61] Hawley to S. Adams, April 1, 1776. S. Adams Papers.

[62] S. Adams to Hawley, April 15, 1775. Cushing, *Writings of S. Adams, op. cit.*, III, 277.

were designed delays and baulks by the People of New York government. Pray Spare no expence or Costs. . . . Let us carry it through or die in it. If we are not wanting to ourselves We shall get through with it. Canada, Canada is the Object."[63] Like a good many New Englanders he was suspicious of New Yorkers and was inclined to blame them, at least in part, for the Canadian fiasco. But the thought of abandoning the Canadian expedition never occurred to him, and he adopted an old suggestion of Gerry's that, as the Indians could never be expected to remain neutral, the colonies might do well to employ them against the British regulars.[64] Further reinforcements, he urged upon Washington several times, could be obtained by sending to Canada the five Continental regiments which were cooling their heels in Boston.[65] While he saw again the unpleasant prospect that New England might be cut off from the other colonies, he felt certain that Massachusetts militia would prove adequate for defense within that province and that the Continentals could be spared for the northern frontier. But Canada gradually became a lost hope even to Hawley, and he turned to the more general problems of defense.

Leaders in the province had long been concerned with procuring and manufacturing gunpowder, and early had tried to stimulate its production. Late in 1775 Hawley had written to Adams that the art of making saltpetre was "well investigated" and that by spring the colony ought to have an adequate supply.[66] By May of the next year he could report that the mills were beginning to produce and also that a large shipment had recently arrived from Bordeaux.[67] He sent directions for making saltpetre to his son

[63] Hawley to S. Adams, May 22, 1776. S. Adams Papers.
[64] Hawley to Gerry, June 2-6, 1776. S. Adams Papers.
[65] Hawley to Washington, June 21, 1776. J. Sparks, *Correspondence of the Am. Revolution.* I, 229.
[66] Hawley to S. Adams, Nov 12, 1775. S. Adams Papers.
[67] *Ibid.*, May 17, 1776. S. Adams Papers.

Joseph Clarke, and told him also of the possibilities of making it at a profit, particularly as there was a state bounty.[68]

Although the Canadian expedition ended in disaster, the remnant of the army which had fallen back to Ticonderoga and Crown Point had to be supported if Sir Guy Carleton were not to be successful in his invasion of the colonies by way of Lake Champlain.[69] Great energy was being expended in New England to secure reinforcements, for Ticonderoga especially, and also for the army at New York. Hawley was chairman of the committee to raise troops in Hampshire County, which were to be part of two regiments sent by Massachusetts. His correspondence that summer was filled with the difficulties that hampered military operations both then and throughout the war.

While in mid-July he could feel that levies in his county were being raised successfully because some towns had already completed their quotas, he was greatly embarrassed by the desire of many recruits to be inoculated with smallpox before marching, an incident which would considerably delay their departure. When one recalls the ravages smallpox had already made in the northern army, one's sympathy is aroused for the men. To march without inoculation meant almost certain contraction of the dread disease and possibly a horrible death in the wilderness far from home. Small wonder that the men hesitated. On the other hand if inoculation were permitted the necessary delay might have grave military consequences. Hawley for once was puzzled and wrote to the Massachusetts Council for advice. He was also perplexed by the absence of instructions for the route to be taken by the Hampshire troops. Furthermore at Number 4 (Charlestown, N. H.) it was rumored that there was no one to pay mileages and

[68] Hawley to Joseph Clarke, April 4, 1776. Hawley Papers II.

[69] Part of Carleton's eventual failure was the result of the energy of Benedict Arnold who built a fleet and weakened Carleton's line of communication.

## A LEADER OF MASSACHUSETTS 165

deliver rations to the men.⁷⁰ The council, quite naturally, was anxious to have the reinforcements on the march as quickly as possible, for soon Carleton would be pushing down the lake and there would be little time for inoculation. The council gave the assurance, however, that smallpox had so far disappeared at Crown Point that the commander of the reinforcements who himself had not had the disease did not choose to be inoculated.⁷¹

When the troops began to set out in late July the route was still unsettled. Since no specific orders had been given, the Hampshire troops were inclined to march by way of Bennington instead of by way of Number 4; rumors of the prevalence of smallpox at the New Hampshire post and of scanty provisions there made them only more determined. How to avoid the plague was the chief thought, and as Hawley wrote, "the men will run the risk of going with but little ammunition, rather than run the risk of the smallpox . . ." His work was more arduous because the field-officers of the battalion were down with smallpox and the county committee had to handle the entire business. Finally, as if to complete his dilemma, he had suddenly been instructed to raise a force of 1500 additional men in the county, but had been supplied with no funds for the purpose.⁷² In the midst of this muddle he was considerably dismayed when all the kettles and canteens for a Berkshire battalion which a little before had marched for New York were dumped down at his house; in a moment of irritation he wrote sarcastically to the council something about "the ruinous fashion of leaving business to execute itself."⁷³ Time did not clear up the difficulties. Some companies when ready marched by way of Bennington, others by way

⁷⁰ Hawley to Mass. Council, July 13, 1776. Mass. Archives, CXCV, 103.
⁷¹ Mass. Council to Hawley, July 15, 1776. Mass. Archives, CXCV, 423.
⁷² Hawley to Mass. Council, July 23, 1776, Force, *op. cit.*, 5th Ser., Vol. I, p. 552.
⁷³ Hawley to Council, July 31, 1776. Mass. Archives CXCV, 161.

of Number 4; some men were inoculated against orders; blankets were lacking for the staff-officers, and with the coming on of the harvest, chances of further successful recruiting became extremely uncertain.[74] The council was, of course, doing its best in an intolerable situation; it was sorry for mistakes but hoped that the Hampshire committee would "cause the men to march to Ticonderoga with all possible dispatch."

By mid-August Hawley had raised successfully five companies of about 700 men and sent them on their way towards Ticonderoga. He wrote to General Gates who was in command at the fortress that he had done everything in his 'power to suppress the pernicious and iniquitous practice of delaying the march of officers and soldiers for the sake of taking the small-pox" and wished him "health, victory and on every account a happy campaign." But he could not control things outside the county and he was soon the recipient of a letter from Gates who was suffering tortures because of the slowness with which troops were joining his army, and particularly because at Number 4, "a villain of a Surgeon" was inoculating the soldiers in the hopes of gaining a few dollars. This doctor deserved in the opinion of the irate general to be thrown into jail; only the distance between him and Gates prevented the culprit from feeling the full weight of the commander's wrath. The Canadian army had been ruined by smallpox and now the militia, serving at great public expense, was tarrying for inoculation while the country lay open to invasion.[75] This letter from Gates caused a considerable sensation; he himself sent a copy to Governor Trumbull of Connecticut, while Hawley sent his to the Council at Watertown whence it passed on to the President of New Hampshire for action. Throughout its course Gates' letter gathered shocked and horrified comments, but by the time the President of New Hamp-

[74] *Ibid.*, Aug. 5, 1776. Mass Archives, CXCV, 170.
[75] Gates to Hawley, Aug. 10, 1776 Mass. Archives, CXCV, 181.

## A LEADER OF MASSACHUSETTS

shire could act at Number 4, the "villain of a Surgeon" must have inoculated the entire army.

In September Hawley was again at Watertown for the meeting of the General Court. Day after day he attended only to public affairs and, harassed by them, was slowly breaking down. Writing to Joseph Clarke that some of the Hampshire militia must be ready to march to Connecticut, he added a hasty word on private affairs, saying, "You must look well to my business for I havent time to think or say a word about it." His time and thoughts were with the army and its none too cheerful winter prospects. He hoped that two-year enlistments could be secured so as to insure some stability. For the troops to the northward snowshoes would be needed, and he wrote several times to Gates of this need, adding that in Northampton he had fifty-nine pairs belonging to the state.[76] The extreme slowness of Congress in paying the soldiers disturbed him; men in Arnold's Canadian expedition were still unpaid and this would have a most unfortunate effect on future enlistments.[77] Visitors returning from the camps under General Gates' command told Hawley of the pitiable conditions among the sick, how doctors were plentiful but medicines lacking. Rations for the able-bodied were limited to meat and bread; no money was available for other provisions. All this made the public mind uneasy. Hawley wrote to Gates for a true account of conditions and for an opinion as to responsibility, whether it rested on Congress or on its fraudulent dishonest agents.[78] These complaints he passed on to Gerry, adding that at Ticonderoga the troops were unpaid and were continually writing to their friends at home for money with which to buy even the necessaries of life.[79]

Gerry was apparently always a willing listener and to him Hawley imparted his many thoughts on military and

[76] Hawley to Gates, Oct. 1, 6, 1776. Force, *op. cit.*, 5th Ser., I, 836, 924
[77] Hawley to Gerry, Sept 11, 1776. S. Adams Papers.
[78] Hawley to Gates, Oct. 6, 1776. Force, *op. cit.*, 5th Ser., I, 924.
[79] Hawley to Gerry, Oct. 13, 1776. S. Adams Papers.

civil matters. The need for guarding the Hudson-Champlain route recurred to him, and he suggested that besides physical obstructions to the passage of an army, stores of artillery and ammunition should be collected at intervals along each side of the river. He also advised the formation of cavalry corps in the American army, for experience was showing clearly this need; military critics of a later day have held that insufficient use of cavalry was one of the weaknesses of Washington's generalship. Hawley recognized that the all-important problem, a rather obvious one, was the raising of an army, for the duration of the war if possible. But the Massachusetts quota of fifteen battalions could be recruited only with great difficulty, despite the twenty-dollar bounty which Congress had at last offered. The great increase in prices made a wage of forty shillings a month highly inadequate, for it bought only a half or a third of what it had a year or two before. Besides, there was the striking contrast between the private soldier and his fellow who enlisted aboard a privateer; the former had a twenty-dollar bounty and forty shillings a month, the latter a share in rich prizes and a pocketful of money. Unless wages continued to rise with prices, wrote Hawley, the plan for raising a standing army was certain to fail. Nevertheless, he urged: "Pray don't let a thought of giving over the case enter our hearts altho this Struggle takes our all, let it go... For God's sake think of it immediately or the Consequences will be tremendous."[80]

Civil matters received attention at times, although never more than a secondary consideration. In mid-summer the question of the Tories had been troublesome. Western Massachusetts was extremely uncertain as to the attitude of the government toward the Tories. Were they to be regarded as traitors? Hawley realized that the Declaration of Independence had made possible the issuing of a proclamation of treason and he hoped against hope that the

[80] *Ibid.*, Oct. 13, 1776. S. Adams Papers.

Continental Congress would take action in order that all those "convicted of endeavoring by overt act to destroy the state, shall be cut off from the earth."[81] Hampshire County loyalists were suspected of communicating with loyalists to the eastward and in New York. Feeling ran high and Hawley desired the Massachusetts Council of Safety to make its attitude clear because people were asserting that they could not "be Safe till some of the Bigg Tories are hanged." To his moderate spirit any such course of action was unthinkable, and he hoped to stave it off.[82]

At Philadelphia that summer of 1776 John Adams was in ill-health and was talking about resignation from the Congress. In a letter to James Warren he suggested a possible successor and insisted that in any case "Major Hawley must be excused no longer."[83] Warren who was in closer contact with Hawley and knew that it would be impossible to persuade him to go to Congress, replied sadly that Hawley's mind was made up and that argument would be futile.[84] Hawley himself probably never considered the idea very seriously; in fact he may not have known of this exchange between Adams and Warren; if he did, it added only one more difficulty to a period of stress and strain.

He reflected a good deal on the work of Congress and its gradual solution of the relations of the central government to the states. But he thought even more of the possibilities that might arise from the meeting between the recently appointed colonial commissioners and Lord Howe; Hawley for one hoped and prayed that the Americans would "not be Cajoled by Lord Howe and carried back into Egypt." He was anxious that the Confederation should be completed and maintained that it should have the power to deter-

[81] *Ibid.*, July 17, 1776. J. T. Austin, *Life of Elbridge Gerry*, I, 207.
[82] Hawley to Mass. Council, July 31, 1776. Mass. Archives, CXCV, 161.
[83] *Warren-Adams Letters*, I, 264.
[84] *Ibid.*, I, 266.

mine the currency in all the states. The states might purchase supplies by borrowing at interest from the Congress.[85] He also believed that Congress should urge all states to support and conform to the types of government already existing among them. After independence had been won, the states could alter and perfect their constitutions at leisure "provided always that they keep them popular, their officers elected by the People and truly republican." On the other hand a refusal to accept the existing systems would produce confusion that might well continue long afterwards and endanger society.[86]

At last Hawley's tremendous activities for the cause, together with his chronic ill-health, broke him. In the late fall of 1776 he left the General Court forever; the rest of his days were to be spent in Northampton. Over-powering melancholy seized him; he seldom left the house, and for hours, smoking furiously he would sit in his great chair before the fire. His eye had a wild and piercing look which might well have frightened all but those who knew him well. Friends like Seth Pomeroy, Doctor Mather or Doctor Hunt would often visit him but their efforts to break through the clouds were seldom successful. Occasionally they persuaded him to ride with them into the meadows or over the beautiful hills beyond the town, but if for a moment they diverted him, he soon fell back into utter gloom. Once after some victory had been won by the Americans, possibly Trenton, Colonel Pomeroy, wrapped in his gorgeous red cloak, called at the house in Pudding Lane. Breaking in on the Major who was still sunk in despondency he cried, "Wake up you cowardly skunk, the day is ours!" Hawley laughed and momentarily the sun shone again. At another time when Hawley expressed to Caleb Strong his fears that the Americans would lose their cause and that he would be executed for his part, Strong assured him that

[85] Hawley to Gerry, Sept. 11, 1776. S. Adams Papers.
[86] *Ibid.*, Oct. 13, 1776. S. Adams Papers.

only a few like Adams and Hancock would suffer. Hawley, greatly aroused, cried out proudly that he would be the first the British would take.[87]

For a year or more he was the victim of this family curse. At times, to be sure, there were lucid intervals and then he would do all in his power to secure men for the army. When orders came periodically for the raising of troops, he frequently addressed them and on one occasion when no one turned out, he marched through the streets of the town escorted by a lone drummer until gradually a procession formed behind him.[88] During such intervals people came as of old to seek his advice on matters of law. Gerry, for a time unaware that the disorder had returned, sent him digests of public affairs. In one of them he returned to their old discussion of the Tories and suggested:"The Tories must be exported: Bonds will not answer the purpose, prisons we have not a Sufficiency, and they are not worth hanging."[89] Samuel Adams told James Warren that a few more of Hawley's "broken hints" would be of great service to him but, however much they might be needed, Hawley was unable to assist.

From his old friend and colleague, James Sullivan, came a delightful letter of sympathy and cheer. In a rhetorical passage Sullivan wrote: "As the ensuing summer will open with the full-blown blossoms of American freedom, and perhaps, by autumn these blooms will be ripened into delicious and permanent fruit, I should think it but just that you should enjoy among your old friends a share of its flavor and therefore hope soon to see you with your usual flow of spirits." He then told Hawley of the arrival of Benjamin Franklin in France and what that was certain to mean for the American cause, how already American cruisers were carrying their prizes into French ports and

[87] From William Bolter's reminiscences. Judd Manuscript, I, 477.
[88] Trumbull, op. cit., II, 423.
[89] Gerry to Hawley, Jan. 1, 1777. Burnet, *op. cit.*, II, 200.

selling them there, adding that the people were in "fine spirits" and that "affairs never looked so promising before." He ended with a wish that Hawley would come to Boston where the sea air and congenial company might well benefit him.[90] It was a good letter, but more than letters were needed to raise Hawley from his slough of despond.

[90] Sullivan to Hawley, Feb. 19, 1777. Hawley Papers II.

CHAPTER IX

RECONSTRUCTION

Hawley's mental breakdown of 1776 was not to be permanent and gradually he had longer and longer periods of clearness. By 1779 he was nearly himself again, though not entirely, for he had lost self-confidence and had fallen behind in the race. New leaders had taken his place and events had run ahead of him. In Hampshire County and Northampton he would always be one of the "river gods," but outside he was already being forgotten. Even at home friendly faces were disappearing. Smallpox had carried off his beloved friend and pastor, John Hooker, and that lifelong colleague in the arts of war and peace, Seth Pomeroy, was asleep in the burying-ground at Peekskill. Somehow it took little time for one to drop behind, and during these years of forced retirement, the world had moved along without him.

Burgoyne had surrendered at Saratoga to the embattled farmers of New York and New England, in fact part of his army had passed through Northampton on its way to Boston. In Pennsylvania and the Jerseys, Washington with his forlorn troops had scurried back and forth for years, seldom winning battles but ever a potential menace and great "mental hazard" to the armies of Howe and Clinton. Now the war had moved to the far-away southern colonies, although there were still two years before Yorktown. Abroad the French alliance which had been only a hope in 1776 had become a fact. The Continental Congress, during the interludes of moving from place to place and carrying on the war, had drawn up a scheme for colonial union, the Articles of Confederation. Possibly they did not establish the "real Continental Covernment" for which Hawley had hoped, but in the circumstances the still unratified Articles were the best arrangement possible. The former colonies and provinces were slowly forming new governments; Massachusetts in 1779 was in the throes of constitution making. A year before the voters had overwhelmingly rejected a constitution prepared by the legislature; possibly a special convention would draw up a more acceptable frame of government.

If his health had permitted, Hawley would without doubt have been one of the leading members of this constitutional convention. His old friends were there; the two Adamses, James Bowdoin and James Sullivan, as well as his former pupils Levi Lincoln and Caleb Strong—only the old "river god" was missing. But while he could not take an active part, he could at least be a keenly interested spectator. Possibly, too, he might have some indirect influence on the decisions of the convention. Caleb Strong, Northampton's delegate, wrote at least once to ascertain Hawley's sentiments and ideas about the questions which confronted the constitution-makers, and Hawley was also in communication with Samuel Adams.[1]

The Northampton man wrote Adams that he was putting forth the small remains of his mental vigor to do his "utmost that all has been done and Suffered Should Not in the end prove abortive." The mission with which the convention was entrusted seemed to him to be of supreme importance, "the framing a Constitution for a great State wherein we are free and at full liberty to make ourselves free to all generations." If this were to be done with any degree of success, the convention ought to take plenty of time, and even if it occupied the best part of a year, this time would be well spent as long as a good constitution resulted.

But more than this. He suggested that when the convention had devised the best model which at the moment it

[1] Strong to Hawley, Oct. 25, 1779. Hawley Papers II.

felt capable of, it should print its plan and send it to all the towns of the state, not for immediate adoption, but for criticism and review. Let everyone, Hawley urged, friend and foe alike, criticize freely; even the delegates to the convention might do well to mull over each phrase and paragraph. Meanwhile, the convention ought not dissolve, but merely stand adjourned. To strengthen his argument, he recalled to Adams the days of their controversies with Francis Bernard and Thomas Hutchinson; how, even when documents had been carefully drawn in sub-committees, edited and gone over paragraph by paragraph in the House, publication had always disclosed some unfortunate defect or blunder. Such a cautious plan, Hawley thought, would more certainly assure adoption because the towns would be less likely to reject the model for some slight triviality if they felt their exceptions had some chance of incorporation in the constitution when the convention reassembled.[2]

Did Adams pay any attention to this letter? We can not know; possibly it is only a coincidence that the method adopted by the convention for securing popular opinion on its work had a resemblance, although distorted, to that suggested by Hawley. Adams was not on the committee which drew up the plan for popular discussion, although James Sullivan was, and Adams may have shown the letter to him, or Hawley may have written to Sullivan in similar vein. At least it is an interesting conjecture.

The convention after working intermittently through the record-breaking cold of that winter of 1779-80 completed its draft of the constitution in March. It then adjourned until June in order that the towns might consider the frame of government, and act through criticism, suggestion, or possible ratification. Actually much of the constitution was devised by Hawley's friend, John Adams, and with the exception of one article, the bill of rights was his work. The mode of ratification adopted by the convention was exceed-

[2] Hawley to Adams, Oct. 18, 1779. S. Adams Papers.

ingly complicated.³ In town meetings the people were to discuss the constitution and vote on it clause by clause, stating objections whenever any article was not favored by a majority. This popular vote was to be tabulated when the convention met again in June. If there appeared a two-thirds majority for every article, the convention was to ratify the constitution; but if such a majority were lacking, the convention before the final ratification was to amend the constitution in accord with the popular will.

Perhaps no town more seriously approached the duty of examining and voting on the constitution than did Northampton; Hawley's part in this examination was all-important. He had slowly resumed his old place in town affairs, acting as moderator at several town meetings even in 1779. At the March elections of the following year he again became a member of the board of selectmen and he was frequently moderator during the consideration of the constitution. For this purpose four town meetings were held between April 24, and May 22. At the first Hawley was chosen to serve on a committee of six to report on the constitution.⁴

This committee's amendments were adopted by the town and assigned to three men, Joseph Hawley, Caleb Strong and one other, for redrafting. Actually the work fell to Hawley as a sub-committee of one, but the work was so unsatisfactory to his colleagues that they refused to present it to the town meeting. Hawley, however, rose in the assembly and moved that his draft be read and considered. His influence was so great that the motion received hearty support. After a long drawn-out session lasting until nearly sundown, Hawley secured the adoption of his amendments and their dispatch to Boston.⁵ His criticism,

³ This has been ably summarized by Professor S. E. Morison in his discussion of the Massachusetts Constitution of 1780 before the Massachusetts Historical Society. See *Mass. Hist. Soc. Proc.*, Ser., III, Vol. L, p. 396.
⁴ Northampton Town Records, April 24, 1780.
⁵ Northampton Town Records, May 22, 1780.

however, had no effect, although an analysis shows that the political theories which he held were based on a surprising soundness of thought and reasoning. Unlike most of his old colleagues, he had not turned away from political liberalism. Indeed he stood apart from the horde of "village Hampdens and Sidneys" who disputed so freely in Massachusetts that gloomy spring.

Much of the Northampton criticism of the constitution may be ignored because it was concerned only with trivialities. On one article, however, it was particularly explicit—on the definition of the franchise for electors of the governor and members of the house of representatives. On this issue all the arguments were used which were to be heard during the struggles for universal manhood suffrage in the next half century; when Massachusetts attempted a revision of its constitution in 1820, no arguments for franchise extension were presented that could not be found in the Northampton proposals of 1780. Thomas Jefferson writing his *Notes on the State of Virginia* in 1781 was to express similar sentiments on these questions.[6] Although ideas of political democracy may have been part of the spirit of the times, they had little influence on most political leaders. The Thomas Jeffersons and Joseph Hawleys were too few and too far apart to be effective at the moment.

The proposed Massachusetts constitution gave the vote to every male citizen possessed of a freehold annually worth £3, or any estate valued at £60. But the Northampton amendment demanded that all males over twenty-one years of age and resident in the state three years should vote for governor and representatives.[7] A restricted franchise, the town maintained, infringed "the natural, essential and inalienable right of many persons" to vote in the choice of representatives. Now, in the convention's address to the

[6] T. Jefferson, *Notes on the State of Va.* (1787), pp. 192, 194.

[7] M. C. Clune, *Joseph Hawley's Criticism of the Constitution of Massachusetts.* p. 18. The manuscript of the Northampton returns is among the Hawley Papers II, and also in the Mass. Archives.

people, it had been stated that representation ought to be founded on the principle of equality, that the house of representatives was intended as representative of persons, the senate of property. But Northampton was unable to understand how there could be any distinction between the senate and the house when chosen by the same electors, no matter how their members might be apportioned to property or to persons. In fact, it would seem that any distinction must depend on the qualifications of the electors, because a restriction of the franchise to persons of some estate, gave property control and representation in both houses.[8]

Furthermore, justice was violated, the Northampton citizens insisted, by excluding the propertyless from voting. Did not the preamble to the Declaration of Rights in the proposed constitution set forth the thesis that "the body politic is formed by a voluntary association of individuals... a social compact, by which the whole people covenants with each citizen, and each citizen with the whole people, that all shall be governed by certain laws for the common good. It is the duty of the people, therefore, in framing a Constitution of Government, to provide for an equitable mode of making laws..."? Certainly it would be presumptuous to expect that the disfranchised would ever agree to be governed by laws in whose making they had no voice; yet such persons were citizens and their disfranchisement contradicted the preamble.[9] A property qualification was also directly contrary to the first article of the Declaration of Rights that "all men are born free and equal and have certain natural, essential, and inalienable rights." If this were true, how could individuals be deprived of their inalienable rights, rights which they could not give away? The violation of this declaration by the disfranchisement of the unpropertied who, nevertheless, were under the

[8] Clune, *op. cit.*, pp. 19-20.
[9] *Ibid.*, p. 21.

jurisdiction and legislation of the General Court, placed them in a condition of absolute slavery.[10]

But when taxes were proposed, the disfranchised were not omitted; whether property owners or not, they were always taxed and forced to bear heavy burdens and render public services. Moreover, since the large property owners always strove to make the proportion of personal taxes as high as possible in order to pay less on their estates, disfranchisement of the unpropertied would only raise this share still farther. The poor might not object to giving property great weight in the legislature; but they would object to being ignored completely, to being considered only as chattels for enumeration, as beasts and nothing more. "Shall these poor polls," asked Northampton, "who have gone for us into the greatest perils, and undergone infinite fatigues in the present war to rescue us from slavery, and had a great hand under God, in making the great salvation in our Land, which is in a great degree wrought out, some of them leaving at home their poor families, to endure the sufferings of hunger and nakedness, shall they now be treated by us like villains or African slaves? God forbid!"[11] As a last and striking point in its indictment of the franchise clause, the town brought forth the time-worn, yet still effective British bogey. For was not this treatment of the propertyless, this exclusion of any vote for the legislature, closely akin to the exclusion of an American voice in parliamentary legislation on American affairs? That had aroused high and just indignation; to perpetuate it seemed hardly fitting in the state which had led in organizing protests against parliamentary supremacy.[12]

Hawley's personal views were expressed in a letter which was intended for publication in the Boston *Independent Ledger*. With able and well-founded objections he attacked the complicated method devised for securing popular

[10] *Ibid.*, p. 24.
[11] *Ibid.*, p. 27.
[12] *Ibid.*, p. 28.

expression on the constitution, a method far more devious than that which he had suggested to Samuel Adams. "I believe," he said, "it will require the industry and distinguishing faculties, of beings superior to the human kind, satisfactory to determine from such returns, what the sentiments are in which . . . two thirds of the people are agreed."[13] Perhaps that was a minor point, but his criticism of the articles of the constitution demands particularly careful attention.

The Declaration of Rights, was not, he thought, made up of indisputable truths set forth in clear and unequivocal language. Instead, its articles were inconsistent and controversial, especially those which dealt with religious matters. Hawley has been called "the only political leader of Revolutionary Massachusetts whose religious views were broad and tolerant"; certainly his career from the time of the Jonathan Edwards controversy had been a steady struggle against clerical infallibility and clerical interference in civil affairs. Massachusetts, at the time, had no Jefferson to fight for religious liberty; Hawley alone of all the old leaders raised his voice for freedom of conscience and his voice by now was carrying little weight. But he questioned the proposition that "it is the right as well as the duty of all men in society, publicly, and at stated seasons, to worship the Supreme Being." He was also uncertain whether "the happiness of a people, and the good order and preservation of civil government, essentially depend upon piety, religion and morality." Article III, the only part of the Declaration of Rights not drawn by John Adams, required public support of religious establishments and was to Hawley's mind not only inconsistent with the inalienable rights of conscience, but so loosely worded as to "afford plenty of that glorious uncertainty, which [was] the source of the emoluments of the men" of

[13] *Ibid.*, p. 39. This letter is reproduced in Clune; the original is in the Hawley Papers II. Apparently it was never published as Hawley had intended.

his profession. He accused its authors of purposely giving the articles a loose and uncertain wording in the attempt to make a religious establishment appear consistent with the rights of conscience.[14]

Many of the other articles in the declaration, he said, were resounding nothings; they reminded him of the doggerel description of the Salem Fair,

"There's a Fair at Salem, a little behind the Hill,
 Where something may be bought, if anything is to sell."

This was especially true of the article which guaranteed life, liberty, and property according to standing laws, except when public exigencies should otherwise require. Hawley saw this as no guarantee at all, as "only a well sounding declaration, rather than a certain, firm and solid foundation of our property, rights and liberties."[15]

Basing his attack on logical deductions from the Declaration of Rights, Hawley also noted many minor defects and contradictions in the frame of government itself. The all-important propositions, he declared, were that "all men are born free and equal" and that they have "certain natural, essential, and inalienable rights." All other articles of the declaration and frame of government should conform with these. So he exhorted the convention to "give over the impossible [task] of endeavoring to make a religious establishment [consistent] with the inalienable Rights of Conscience." Give the people, he urged, a representative in the legislature in whose choice all competent and capable of voting shall have a voice; "let every adult freeman have a right to vote for the Governour." Such provisions would only be "doing proper honour and paying due regard to the rights of human nature," while at the same time doing away with the "jargon of a virtual representation."[16]

[14] *Ibid.*, pp. 40-42.
[15] *Ibid.*, p. 43.
[16] *Ibid.*, pp. 50-51.

Throughout the constitution Hawley found a studied hesitancy to use the term freeman "as if it implied that there were slaves in the State." This refusal to recognize the existence of slaves he found cowardly and he for one hated "the inhuman, unjust, and cruel practice of enslaving" his fellowman. The disguise attempted by omitting the word freeman in the constitution, he felt, would "not remove the shame and just reproach—while the iniquitous practice is notorious."[17]

But all this was to no purpose. When the convention reassembled on June 7, it immediately appointed a committee to examine the returns from the towns. Although these men were not "beings superior to the human kind," they miraculously determined that two thirds of the people had voted for the constitution.[18] The convention then ratified the constitution and ordered elections for the new government to be held on the first Monday in September. In these elections Joseph Hawley was elected a senator from Hampshire County and in due course received a writ of summons from the president of the council.

But Hawley was steadfast in his opposition to what he believed to be the illiberal clauses of the new constitution. In a challenging and protesting letter to the senate he declined to take his seat because of the requirement that all members of the General Court must take an oath of belief in the Christian religion. This oath was exacted whether or not a man had previously professed his Christianity and practiced Christian teachings. To Hawley, the value of the oath was debatable, and he sarcastically queried: "Did our Father Confessors imagine, that a man who had not so

[17] *Ibid.*, pp. 51-52. In this regard it may be worth recalling that soon after the adoption of the constitution slavery was abolished in Massachusetts as the result of judicial interpretation of the "free and equal" clause in the Declaration of Rights.

[18] Professor S. E. Morison has challenged this vote in a discussion before the Massachusetts Historical Society, tending to prove that the constitution never was ratified by a majority of the voters. See *Mass. Hist. Soc. Pro.* Ser., III, Vol. L, p. 376.

much fear of God in his heart, as to restrain him from acting dishonestly and knavishly in the trust of a Senator or representative would hesitate a moment to subscribe that declaration." The required profession also contradicted the inalienable rights of an individual as well as the article of the Declaration guaranteeing the right to "elect officers and to be elected, for public employments." In conclusion Hawley wrote:

By the Constitution of the Commonwealth of Massachusetts I am, may it please your Honors one of the Senators and I strongly disposed according to my poor abilities, to execute the duties of my office but [by] the unconscionable not to say dishonorable terms established by the same constitution, I am barred from endeavoring to perform the duties. I have been a professed Christian nearly 40 years, and altho' I have been guilty of many things unworthy of that character whereof I am ashamed; yet I am not conscious that I have been guilty of anything wholly inconsistent with the truth of that profession. The laws under the first charter required of the subjects of that State in order to their enjoying some privileges that they should be members in full communion of some Christian Church. But it never was before required in the Massachusetts Bay that a subject in order to his enjoying or exercising any Franchise or office should make profession of the Christian Religion before a temporal court.[19]

As a result of his refusal to serve, Hampshire County lacked full representation in the senate during the first session of the new General Court, and at the first regular state election in the succeeding April the county failed to elect its full number of senators. Constitutionally, therefore, an election had to be made by a joint ballot of the senate and house of representatives. Their choice fell on Joseph Hawley. Once again he declined to serve; not by way of protest this time, but rather because of his old enemy, ill-health. "My wishes to serve my Country are as ardent as ever," he wrote, "Would to God that my

[19] Hawley to Mass. Senate, Oct. 28, 1780. *Mass. Hist. Soc. Pro.*, Ser., III, Vol. LIX, p. 79. Also printed in H. Niles', *Principles and Acts of the Rev.*, p. 374.

Strength and Capacity were equally so!" The memory of the miseries into which intense application to state business had cast him before was too fresh to make public service attractive.[20] It was a great loss to Massachusetts and one may well wonder if the events of the next few years would not have been a little happier if Hawley had been serving in the General Court.

It was not an easy time anywhere, but western Massachusetts in particular was beginning to feel the effects of the long war. The continued recruiting had drained off men enough to hinder farming; requisitions for horses, beef, and grain came with irritating and increasing frequency; while constant taxation and the depreciation of currency, amounting to what was actually a forced loan, were driving many to the verge of bankruptcy. Out of this situation and the breakdown of social organization inevitably attendant on a revolution came the riots and disturbances which eventually culminated in Shays' Rebellion. At Northampton, town meetings were called frequently to answer the steady demands for the sinews of war—men and supplies, and at these meetings in spite of his ill-health, Joseph Hawley was moderator as well as one of the selectmen.[21]

During the early years of the Revolution, county conventions had met to discuss and resolve questions of general public interest; this method of expressing public opinion had been continued. Now that the war was nearly over, the conventions turned to the pressing problems of financial instability and impending bankruptcy. The time and the place were ready for the demagogue; the conventions provided a ready-made audience. The first county convention of this period to attract much attention was held across the river from Northampton, at Hadley, on February 11, 1782. What occurred there is uncertain, but a demagogue

[20] Hawley to Mass. Senate, June 8, 1781. Mass. Archives, CCIII, 313.
[21] Northampton Town Records, 1781.

## RECONSTRUCTION 185

appeared in the person of one Samuel Ely from the hill town of Conway. Apparently he talked too much, because before the noise of the convention had died away he was "examined by Major Hawley for treasonable practices." One of the local divines, recording the convention in his diary, added the comment: "Government seems to be endangered by noise of people in debt."[22] The next month another convention met at Hatfield, and Hawley headed the delegates from Northampton.[23] The discussions covered all the burdens under which the people of the region were laboring. The convention was especially opposed to the holding of the county court where prosecutions for debt would undoubtedly be entered. Although the Northampton delegates were against all radical measures, their opposition availed nothing and civil war began to threaten. During the sitting of the Court of General Sessions of the Peace at Northampton in April, Samuel Ely was the leader of mobs which at various times attempted to close the court. Fortunately a guard of former soldiers and militia was at hand to protect the court house. Before long Ely was arrested and bound over for appearance at the following session of the Superior Court.[24]

A few days after Ely's attempt to break up the court at Northampton, Hawley wrote a vivid explanation of the disturbances to Ephraim Wright, one of Northampton's representatives in the legislature. Cautious still, and, still loving order, he was not so blind as to be unable to see the fundamental causes of the distress and dissatisfaction which were so prevalent in Hampshire County. But, as always, he had a good deal of sympathy for those who complained of ill treatment and of injustice. Much of the "great and growing uneasiness" in the county, he wrote, was due to "the Government's Securities being made

[22] Diary of Jonathan Judd, Feb. 14, 1782. Quoted in Judd Manuscript, Revolutionary Matters.
[23] Northampton Town Records, March 11, 1782.
[24] Trumbull, *op. cit.*, II, 456.

payable at very distant times." As these securities had been given in payment for services long since past, and times were hard, people were anxious to realize on their certificates. But the securities were valueless either for cash payments or for taxes. Furthermore, Continental soldiers had been paid with these securities which now were little more than so much worthless paper in their hands. "You cant hear them Speak of this matter," Hawley wrote, "but in rage and flame, besides there is, as the old three years continentals Say about three months of their Service ... for which there never has been any allowance." But he warned, "they are a fierce set of men, and the Government will find, *you may rely upon it* that the Government will find, that these People, unless they are speedily Satisfied on these Two heads will in these parts pay no Taxes and there will not be men enough here to compel them to do it." Yet these men had done real service in the war although they had never received anything therefor except worthless paper money and the government securities which in many instances they had been obliged to sell for almost nothing to sharpers. In spite of their ill treatment these old Continentals had defended the inferior court against "the Mobb which Ely brought to town." In Hawley's opinion unless some relief were given speedily, the loyalty of the old soldiers and poorer people could not long be relied upon.

As a result of the war people were living in poverty, unable to pay their public or private debts. When attempts were made to collect these debts in court, the poor debtor found his position made worse by the addition of the costs of court. Hawley in his letter to Wright pointed out that at the recent sitting of the Court of Common Pleas there were "two hundred and twenty one actions for the recovery of debts where the defendant did not at all Contest the debt. The Bills of Cost in three quarters of that number of cases, without any appeal will exceed forty shillings. The Jurors attended three days and had but three cases put to them in the whole."[25]

Out of such conditions Ely and his kind were gathering supporters and sympathizers, for the disturbances were only beginning. When the Superior Court met early in May, it found Ely guilty, sentenced him to six months imprisonment, and fined him £50. Soon however, the discontented elements decided to rescue Ely from the Springfield jail where he was imprisoned. On June 12 they appeared suddenly in force, and as most of the men of the town were at Longmeadow for the funeral of the Reverend Stephen Williams, easily broke open the jail. This act aroused the conservative citizens and before long more than 1000 men formed a posse under the high sheriff of the county to hunt down the mob and Ely. When the representatives of the law came up with the insurgents, hostilities were avoided by a conference between the two groups. Ultimately an agreement was signed by which three hostages were given until Ely, who had fled from his own supporters, should be returned to jail. Meanwhile the unpleasantness of a heavy rain had cooled the enthusiasm of the mob, most of which dispersed. Thus a direct settlement was avoided for the moment.[26]

Hawley was greatly disturbed by the "alarming situation" and wrote for aid to John Hancock who was now governor. At the moment of his writing, all was quiet, but the mob might collect again, as it actually did a few days later. Hawley gave all honor to the sheriff and his men, but since the posse had disbanded he feared for the future; particularly was he disturbed by the prospect of internecine warfare. The rioters were constantly threatening to destroy the Northampton jail and to burn the town; who could tell when they might not turn words into deeds? More distressing perhaps than this was the difficulty of defending the town. Men could hardly fight

[25] Hawley to Ephraim Wright, April 16, 1782. Hawley Papers, II.
[26] Trumbull, op.cit., II, 460.

against friends, acquaintances and brothers. "I will Venture to say," wrote Hawley "that the Prowess of the People of this town is equal to that of any Town in the State, but it is next to impossible for us to defend ourselves against these our Brethren, because we cannot fight them. Though their numbers are greater than ours that does not principally intimidate us, but to meet our Enemy who is determined to fight us, who may not be resisted unto blood and death, is a case Extremely Singular."[27] Soon after Ely was given up, and temporarily the scene in Hampshire County became more placid.

Meanwhile the General Court had suspended the writ of habeas corpus in the county and appointed a committee to investigate the cause of the disturbances. Hawley had proposed such a committee in a letter to the General Court and had seconded it in a letter to Caleb Strong, at the moment a member of the legislature. Unless some such step should be taken, he wrote, the situation might threaten the entire American cause, for the insurgent spirit was spreading rapidly and infecting all walks of life. "The Gen Court have not had any affair of greater magnitude before them since the Revolution." The committee, he suggested, should consist of "sensible, honest, cool and Patient men" who could explain what had become of the enormous tax assessments. Some of the insurgents were asserting "that it cost them much to maintain the Great men under Geo. 3d but vastly more under the Commonwealth and Congress. We have had it Hurra'd for Geo. 3d within 8 rods of the Court House." This suspicion of Tory and British influence had become almost an obsession with Hawley. He had heard, he wrote Strong, that people were "perpetually taught that they were horribly deceived and deluded by those who first contended with Bernard and Hutchinson ... that they were the

[27] Hawley to John Hancock, June 14, 1782. Mass Archives. CCIV, 159.

men who brought all their burdens upon them." But as usual Hawley had the spirit of moderation and urged that the committee must "go in to the towns and learn the facts on the spot, by seeing and hearing, and neglect of this may deceive and ruin the government."[28]

The committee, which included Samuel Adams, arrived at Northampton in the latter part of July. It was the last time Adams and Hawley were to be associated in public service. Working among the people and with a convention which met at Hatfield on August 7, they achieved a calming of passions that continued until the final outburst of four years later when men went out with Shays. But in 1782 the situation had been serious and the legislature had good reason to thank the committee "for their indefatigable and successful endeavors in so great a degree quieting the disturbances that had arisen in the county."[29]

There was a year more of active work for Joseph Hawley. In 1783 he served his last term as selectman and although still moderator of town meetings he dropped out of committee work.[30] Conventions still continued to meet in the county but they were more conservative than in the previous year. Such were those which Hawley attended at Hatfield in March and April, 1783. Of the first Jonathan Judd wrote: "We were good Natured, had no Disputes, very reserved. They want to get rid of Major Hawley and myself."[31] The mobs which gathered during court sittings in the summer were easily dispersed, although their economic grievances were unredressed. Meanwhile, the signing of peace between the former colonies and the mother country had been celebrated at Northampton with "decent mirth and hilarity." Perhaps this would bring the longed-for prosperity, law and order.

[28] Hawley to Caleb Strong, June 24, 1782. Hawley Papers II.
[29] *Mass. Acts and Resolves*, 1782, p. 279.
[30] Northampton Town Records, 1783.
[31] Diary of Jonathan Judd, quoted in Trumbull, *op. cit.*, II, 469.

## Chapter X

## AT THE LAST

The clouds were now gathering fast and Joseph Hawley would never again take part in town or state affairs. Worn out by the storm and stress of the war and its aftermath, he broke down physically and mentally. The old tortures returned, the tortures of religious doubt, the apprehensions of poverty, the hell of complete mental collapse; he became a confirmed invalid. His own generation was passing from the scene; some had preceded him into the next world, others were too busy to think of their old colleague and his sufferings. John Adams was beyond the sea, vainly seeking a commercial treaty between the American Republic and Great Britain. Samuel Adams, and Bowdoin, and Gerry, and Hancock were embroiled in state politics. There was no Seth Pomeroy to cheer him, and James Sullivan had given up all hope of his friend's recovery.

In 1786, the rebellion, which Hawley had been so fearful of three years before, flamed up in Massachusetts. Riotous mobs closed the courts in many parts of the state, and when the snow was deep upon the ground, Captain Daniel Shays with a band of the disaffected tried to capture the arsenal at Springfield. Hampshire County was aroused, Northampton not the least, but the old "river god" was no longer interested in civil tumults. Nursed and attended by the ever-devoted Mercy, Hawley lived on, although his life was over. Few beams of light pierced the gloom as weeks and months became years. Outside, the state and nation were assuming form and stability but of all this the old leader was unaware. Thomas Cushing, his former associate, died in the late winter of 1788, and though Joseph

AT THE LAST 191

Hawley never learned of this, it was one more evidence that his generation was passing on. His time had come, also; and on a March day in 1788, all Northampton crowded into the meeting house to do him final honor. The Lord had taken "away from Jerusalem—from Judah the stay and staff, the mighty man, the counsellor and the eloquent orator."[1] But Joseph Hawley had found peace.

When a few days later his will was opened, the town learned that even death could not end his service. He had bequeathed some 800 acres of land in Pelham to Northampton for the support of a school, a school to be "maintained in a Steady and liberal manner and by faithful and able masters taught and instructed." Throughout his busy, varied life Hawley had taken a regular interest in the town's schools and in learning; possibly his little fortune now would aid in "the good education of the Successive generations of the lads of Northampton." Above all, as he had written, the bequest was inspired by the wish to benefit "the Town where I was born and lived most of my days, and which has Seen fit from the early days of my Manhood, to honour me with many instances of their respect esteem and confidence."[2] Sometime later the town set up a school as a monument to its benefactor and loyal servant. Today, nearly a century and a half afterward, there is still a Hawley Grammar School, "maintained in a Steady and liberal manner," but only the searchers of historical dustbins remember Major Joseph Hawley.

Something, possibly his chronic ill-health, prevented Joseph Hawley from achieving a place among the immortals of the American Revolution. His contemporaries believed him to be a great man; friend and foe alike attributed to him wisdom, leadership, and a fine sense of justice. In 1776, he could have had any honor within the gift of Massachusetts and men hoped that he would go to

[1] *Hampshire Gazette* (Northampton), March 19, 1788.
[2] Will of Joseph Hawley in Probate Records of Hampshire County.

the Continental Congress. Instead he gave in to invalidism and retired. Even this does not seem a convincing reason for his leaving the scene when there was still so much to be done. Was it because of a sense of false modesty? Some of his contemporaries have suggested it. Or was it because of an inability to be the complete partisan, as Thomas Hutchinson thought? Certainly it cannot have been because of a growing conservatism; the worst excesses of the Revolution were already passed, and he remained a liberal. Probably there can be no satisfactory explanation; one can only regret that the new nation had to be deprived of the steady counsel that might have been afforded by Joseph Hawley.

During his lifetime he had seen the American colonies, Massachusetts in particular, grow from childhood into lusty adolescence. He had helped in the removal of the old French and Indian menace. The growth of religious liberalism had been in tune with his spirit. Economic, social and political developments were all reflected in his own life; all of them he saw and much of them he was. Then like Moses of old he was denied the final realization of his work; but unlike the Hebrew leader he never really saw the promised land.

There is tragedy in the career of Joseph Hawley, the tragedy of genius cut off before its time and the tragedy of unrecognized contribution. An "empty barrel" like John Hancock is among the Fathers; so are unscrupulous partisans like Samuel Adams and Elbridge Gerry, but Joseph Hawley's praises are unsung. Perhaps he was not a great man, perhaps he was not a great personality; but if that be true, his contemporaries misjudged him. The modesty that was his in life followed his name after life had departed. Later generations forgot him and he became only a modest footnote on the page of history; there were no children to rise up and call him blessed. So today Joseph Hawley, almost forgotten, sleeps under the pines in the peace and quiet of God's acre.

## BIBLIOGRAPHY

The materials for a study of Joseph Hawley are not numerous. Except for the collection of family papers, the career of the "river god" must be followed in the public records of his time and in the correspondence of his contemporaries. Most secondary works concerned with his period contain but incidental reference to Joseph Hawley and can be used only to obtain the scene in which the man moved. The following bibliography is in no way a complete list of the sources consulted in the preparation of this life. It does include, however, the works cited in the footnotes and enough general works to supply the background of the period. I have given with a few words of evaluation only those general works which were of most use to me. Students of eighteenth-century New England will immediately recall the most important omissions; for these I have no excuse other than the practical limitations of a useful bibliography.

### Manuscript Sources

Samuel Adams Papers, 1653-1803. (New York Public Library). This vast collection contains not only the correspondence of Adams with many of the Revolutionary leaders, but considerable correspondence between Hawley and Elbridge Gerry.

Hampshire County Records.
*Minute Book of Court of General Sessions of the Peace and Inferiour Court of Common Pleas*, 1746-1766. Vols. 5-8;
*Minute Book of Court of Common Pleas*, 1766-1780. Vols. 9-11.

## 194  BIBLIOGRAPHY

*Minute Book of Court of General Sessions of the Peace*, 1766-1789. Vols. 10-11. (Hampshire County Court House, Northampton, Mass.). In using these records, one is handicapped by the absence of any index of the attorneys in the suits, although the cases are excellently catalogued.

*Superior Court of Judicature*, 1750-1774. (In Suffolk County Court House, Boston, Mass.). The records are well kept, but the attorneys in the suits are not mentioned in the minutes of the case. As a result, one must know the name of the defendant or the appellant in the suit to find the record of the case; the name of the attorney must be found in the records of the lower courts.

*Probate Records of Hampshire County* (Northampton). Here will be found the will of Joseph Hawley 2nd, and the inventory of his estate; also the will of Major Joseph Hawley; the inventory of his estate has apparently been lost.

HAWLEY PAPERS (New York Public Library). The principal part of this collection is in two boxes, originally volumes, in the Bancroft Collection. The first box contains many papers dealing with public and private affairs from 1653 to 1774 and also some notes by George Bancroft. The second is made up of general correspondence and the papers of the Northampton Committee of Safety. Unfortunately at the present time only part of the collection is indexed and none of it is in very good condition. There are also a couple of bundles of miscellaneous Hawley papers containing a few letters, deeds and odd notes.

*Massachusetts Archives*, Vols. 25, 58, 79, 96, 193, 195, 203, 204 (State House, Boston). In these volumes are to be found many of the letters which passed between Joseph Hawley and the provincial authorities. The collection is especially valuable for the period of the Revolution. In certain instances other letters contain pointed references to Hawley. Most of the volumes are well indexed.

HUTCHINSON CORRESPONDENCE (New York Public Library). A collection of transcripts made for George Bancroft. A good deal of the correspondence between Thomas Hutchinson and Israel Williams is included, duplicating in part the material in the Israel Williams Papers in the collection of the Massachusetts Historical Society.

JUDD MANUSCRIPT (Forbes Library, Northampton). About sixty volumes and 1,000 loose pieces composing a vast collection of miscellaneous information about Northampton, its leading personalities and about the Connecticut Valley. To a large extent it is composed of extracts from town and county records, from diaries and journals, of personal reminiscences and observation. Unfortunately the collection as a whole is inadequately indexed and is difficult to use because of the original compiler's lack of organization. Much of the material in the Judd Manuscript is quoted or reprinted in J. R. Trumbull's History of Northampton Mass.

NORTHAMPTON.
*Northampton Town Records*, 1653-1801. 3 vols. (Northampton). Includes records of the precinct meetings until 1753 and of the town meetings. In most instances the records of the meetings are only brief minutes.

*Northampton Town Records* (Massachusetts Historical Society). For the colonial period this collection largely duplicates the one at Northampton.

*Proprietors Records, Town of Northampton*, 1757-1778 (Northampton). Brief minutes of the meetings of the town proprietors.

# BIBLIOGRAPHY

*Northampton Town Records, Births, Deaths and Marriages.* These are excellently cared for and indexed.

*Records of the First Church of Northampton,* Book I, 1661-1846. For the eighteenth century these records are very thin and make no notice of the Edwards affair except to record the pastor's dismissal.

*Documents Manuscripts and Autographs Relating to or written by General Seth Pomeroy 1706-1777* (Forbes Library, Northampton). A beautifully bound and mounted volume of Pomeroy manuscripts. Many of them are of little more than antiquarian interest, although there is considerable material on colonial social, economic, and political life.

JOURNALS OF SETH POMEROY (Forbes Library, Northampton). These cover the Louisbourg expedition of 1745 and the Lake George expedition of 1755. They are both printed in Trumbull's History of Northampton and with many of the items in the Pomeroy papers are printed in The Journals and Papers of Seth Pomeroy, edited by L. E. de Forest.

WASHBURN MANUSCRIPTS (Massachusetts Historical Society). A collection of miscellaneous papers relating to Massachusetts history. Contains one letter from Thomas Hancock to Hawley.

ISRAEL WILLIAMS PAPERS (Massachusetts Historical Society). A large collection of letters and documents relating to eighteenth-century Massachusetts. The letters between Thomas Hutchinson and Israel Williams are particularly valuable for their comments on the rôle played by Joseph Hawley.

DIARY OF STEPHEN WILLIAMS July 18, 1745-Jan. 1749 (Massachusetts Historical Society). A diary kept by the minister of Longmeadow, Mass. while he was chaplain of one of the Massachusetts regiments on the Louisbourg expedition.

# BIBLIOGRAPHY

## PRINTED SOURCES

*Acts and Resolves of the Province of Massachusetts Bay* 1747-1776. 21 vols. Boston, 1869-1922. These printed collections of the many legislative acts and resolves contain considerable material relating to the public service of Joseph Hawley.

ADAMS, C. F., The Works of John Adams, 10 vols. Boston, 1856. Include not only Adams' vast correspondence but also his diary and autobiography, together with a memoir by Charles Francis Adams.

BACKUS, I., History of New England with particular reference to the Baptists. 2 vols. Newton Mass., 1871. A contemporary's famous account of the struggle of the Baptists for religious liberty.

*Bibliothecra Sacra and Theological Review*, Vol. I. Andover, 1844. Reprints a letter from Jonathan Edwards to Hawley reviewing Hawley's part in the church controversy, together with a brief biographical sketch of Hawley, pp. 579-91.

BLISS, GEORGE, An Address to the Members of the Bar of Hampshire, Franklin and Hampden. Springfield, 1827. A gossipy account of the early Hampshire County bar and its members by a man who had known most of the early leaders.

Boston *Gazette*, 1772, 1773.

Boston *Evening Post*, 1767-1768. The issues for Jan. 5, July 6, July 13, print Hawley's replies to "Philanthrop" on the Berkshire Affair.

BRADFORD, ALDEN, Speeches of the Governors of Massachusetts from 1765 to 1775 and the Answers of the House of Representatives to the same. Boston, 1818. A valuable collection of the most important documents illustrating the growing disagreement between the governor and the legislature. It is difficult to use as there is no index. Usually cited as *Mass. State Papers*.

BURNETT, E. C., Letters of Members of the Continental Congress, 4 vols. Washington 1921-1928. An exceedingly valuable collection of letters relating to the Revolution and containing some of the correspondence which passed between Hawley and the members of the Massachusetts delegation at Philadelphia.

*Centennial Gazette* (Northampton, 1876). A special edition of the regular *Hampshire Gazette* devoted principally to a picture of Northampton in 1776. Contains a good deal of miscellaneous but useful information.

CLUNE, M. C., Joseph Hawley's Criticism of the Constitution of Massachusetts. Smith College Studies in History, Vol. III, No. I. Northampton, 1917. Reprints Hawley's able criticism, the original of which is in the Hawley Papers, II. A brief biographical sketch of Hawley precedes the document.

CUSHING, H. A., The Writings of Samuel Adams. 4 vols. New York, 1908. Some of the letters which passed between Samuel Adams and Hawley are included in this collection.

DEXTER, F. B., Documentary History of Yale University 1701-1745. New Haven, 1916. A very useful collection of documents relating to the early history of Yale.

DWIGHT, S. E., The Life of President Edwards. New York, 1830. Although ostensibly a biography, the book reproduces so much of Edwards' journal and correspondence as to be practically a collection of sources.

DWIGHT, TIMOTHY, Travels in New England and New York. 4 vols. London, 1823. Vol. I contains a brief estimate of Hawley as this famous president of Yale knew him.

EDWARDS, JONATHAN. A Faithful Narrative of the Surprizing Work of God in the Conversion of many Hundred Souls in Northampton, of New England, etc. Boston, 1738. A vivid account of the revival at Northampton in 1735. Edwards describes the suicide of Joseph Hawley's father.

FORCE, PETER, American Archives. 4th series, Vol. IV, V; 5th series, Vol. I, II. Washington 1843-1851. A great but uncompleted collection of source material for the American Revolution. Contains much of Hawley's correspondence with the leaders in Philadelphia and Boston. The index is not wholly reliable.

*Hampshire Gazette.* The issue for March 19, 1788 carries a notice of Hawley's death and funeral. The issue for June 15, 1852 has a brief biographical sketch of Hawley's mother written by Sylvester Judd.

*Journal of the Honorable House of Representatives at a Great or General Court of the Massachusetts-Bay in New England.* 1754-1756, 1765-1774, 1776-1777. Printed in Boston at the end of each session. The volumes are not easy to use as they are unindexed. As they are only journals, the record of debates is left to one's imagination.

*Journals of Each Provincial Congress of Massachusetts in 1774 and 1775 and of the Committee of Safety.* Boston, 1838. An extremely useful and valuable volume; well-indexed.

*Journals of the Continental Congress* 1774-1783. 25 vols. Washington, 1904-1922.

*Journal of the Convention for framing a Constitution of Government for the State of Massachusetts Bay, Sept. 1, 1779 to June 16, 1780.* Boston, 1832. Essential for any understanding of the work behind the Massachusetts Constitution of 1780.

MACDONALD, WILLIAM, Select Charters and Other Documents Illustrative of American History, 1606-1775. New York, 1899.

MAYHEW, EXPERIENCE, Grace Defended in a Modest Plea for an Important Truth. Boston, 1744. The extremely interesting theological work which undermined Hawley's orthodox beliefs.

*Massachusetts Acts and Resolves,* 1782-1783. Boston, 1782 (Reprinted 1890). This volume contains some material concerning the riots in Hampshire in 1782.

NILES, H., Principles and Acts of the Revolution. Baltimore 1822. A useful collection of Revolutionary documents including Joseph Hawley's "Broken Hints."

POMEROY, SETH, JOURNALS AND PAPERS OF, edited by L. E. de Forest, Society of Colonial Wars in the State of New York. 1926. Contains the journals of Seth Pomeroy for the Louisbourg expedition of 1745 and the Lake George expedition of 1755, together with considerable miscellaneous material concerning eighteenth-century life in Northampton. Originals of these documents are in the Forbes Library, Northampton.

SEWALL, SAMUEL, DIARY OF, 3 vols. In Mass. Hist. Soc· Coll. Series 5, Vols., V-VII. A famous diary covering many phases of life in seventeenth and early eighteenth century Massachusetts.

SPARKS, JARED, The Works of Benjamin Franklin. 10 vols. Boston, 1844-1848. This collection in spite of its faults includes some letters covering the period when Franklin was the Massachusetts agent in London which are not found in the standard collection edited by Albert Henry Smyth.

SPARKS, JARED, Correspondence of the American Revolution. 4 vols. Boston, 1853. Like all of the sources edited by Sparks, this has been "polished" by the editor. Volume I contains a letter from Hawley to Washington.

WALE, WILLIAM, editor, George Whitefield's Journals. London, 1905.

WARREN-ADAMS LETTERS. 2 vols. Massachusetts Historical Society Collections. Boston 1917-1925. Chiefly the correspondence between John Adams, Samuel Adams and James Warren, 1743-1814.

## GENERAL HISTORICAL WORKS

ADAMS, J. T., Revolutionary New England, 1691-1776. Boston, 1923. The best single volume on the period although the author is not very friendly toward New England and overemphasizes the theory of economic determinism.

New England in the Republic, 1776-1850. Boston, 1926. This has most of the faults of the previous volume but few of its virtues.

BANCROFT, GEORGE, History of the United States. 10 vols. Boston, 1861. Bancroft must be used with caution since he was writing as a patriotic, democratic historian and is often inexact in the use of quotations. Yet for the period of the Revolution he has a great deal of material that is not to be found elsewhere. Most of his quotations from Hawley's writings are incorrect both in wording and in sequence.

BARRY, J. S., The History of Massachusetts. 3 vols. Boston 1856. An adequate history of the state considering the period in which it was written.

BRADFORD, ALDEN, History of Massachusetts 1764-1789. 2 vols. Boston, 1822-1825. Intended to continue the history of the Commonwealth from the point where Thomas Hutchinson had dropped it. Extremely unreadable although it has the virtue of being based largely on the records.

CHANNING, EDWARD. History of the United States. 6 vols. New York, 1905-1925. The best history of the United States. Vols. II and III cover the story of eighteenth-century Massachusetts.

HART, A. B., editor, Commonwealth History of Massachusetts. 5 vols. New York, 1927-1930. A coöperative work with all the faults but many of the advantages of that type of scholarship. Vols. I and II cover the period between 1689 and 1820.

HOLLAND, J. G., History of Western Massachusetts. 2 vols. Springfield, 1855. An old-fashioned superficial work although with considerable material on local history and personalities not to be found elsewhere.

HUTCHINSON, THOMAS, The History of the Province of Massachusetts Bay. 3 vols. London, 1828. A famous history of Massachusetts written by the next to the last royal governor. The work is, in part, a source; it is based to a considerable extent on sources that have been lost and a good deal is the result of personal contact with the events described.

OSGOOD, H. L., American Colonies in the Eighteenth Century. 4 vols. New York, 1924. The classic study of the institutional history of the American colonies. Represents the best modern scholarship.

PALFREY, J. G., History of New England. 4 vols. Boston, 1883. Although written from the point of view of a Unitarian minister in the Boston of the first half of the nineteenth century this work is still valuable if read with a few grains of salt.

SMITH, J. H., Our Struggle for the Fourteenth Colony. 2 vols. New York 1907. The classic account of the relations between the American Colonies and Canada during the Revolution.

VAN TYNE, C. H., The Causes of the War of Independence. Boston and New York, 1922. An excellent account of the causes of the Revolution.

    The War of Independence: American Phase. Boston and New York, 1929. An excellent account of the Revolution through 1778 although inclined to play up the dark phases of the conflict.

# BIBLIOGRAPHY

WARREN, CHARLES, A History of the American Bar. Boston, 1911. A standard work.

WINSOR, JUSTIN, Narrative and Critical History of North America. 8 vols. Boston, 1887. A famous coöperative work. Somewhat out of date although still very useful.

## BIOGRAPHICAL WORKS

ALDEN, T., A Collection of American Epitaphs. New York, 1814. A series of biographical notices. The sketch of Hawley includes a long extract from the sermon preached at his funeral.

AMORY, T. C., Life of James Sullivan. 2 vols. Boston, 1859. An adequate life of this forgotten friend of Hawley's.

AUSTIN, J. T., The Life of Elbridge Gerry. 2 vols. Boston 1828-1829. Old-fashioned and uncritical biography. Reprints a few of the letters exchanged between Hawley and Gerry.

BRADFORD, ALDEN, Biographical Notices of Distinguished Men in New England. Boston, 1842. A handy volume of sketches of men mostly forgotten, including Joseph Hawley.

Memoir of the Life and Writings of the Reverend Jonathan Mayhew, D.D. Cambridge, 1838.

DEXTER, F. B., Biographical Sketches of the Graduates of Yale College. 6 vols. New York, 1885-1912. Extremely valuable, scholarly work. Contains considerable information about the growth of the college as well.

HISTORICAL SKETCH OF MAJOR JOSEPH HAWLEY OF NORTHAMPTON, MASS. Buffalo, 1890. Reprinted from the *Hawley Record*. Adequate brief sketch of the sort that would appear in a family genealogy.

HOVEY, A., Life and Times of Isaac Backus. Boston, 1859. Gives a good deal of information on the struggle for justice to the Baptists.

SEARS, LORENZO, "Joseph Hawley, the Counsellor of Boston Patriots" (*Magazine of History*, Vol. XX, p. 189). A brief, scholarly article dealing with Hawley's part in the revolutionary movement at Boston.

SHAW, C. L., "Joseph Hawley, the Northampton Statesman" (*Magazine of History*, Vol. XXII, p. 489). A sketch of Hawley which reprints an address purporting to have been given by Hawley to the Northampton minutemen.

TUDOR, WILLIAM, The Life of James Otis. Boston, 1823. An old but still the principal life of Otis.

WELLS, W. V., The Life and Public Services of Samuel Adams. 3 vols. Boston, 1865. A eulogistic biography although valuable for its information on Adams' contemporaries and for the reprinting of much source material.

## LOCAL HISTORIES

ALLEN, W., An Address Delivered at Northampton, Mass., October 29, 1854, in Commemoration of the Close of the Second Century since the Settlement of the Town. Northampton, 1855. A gossipy historical sketch of Northampton.

CHASE, ARTHUR, History of Ware, Massachusetts. Cambridge, 1911.

CLARKE, SOLOMON, Antiquities, Historicals and Graduates of Northampton. Northampton, 1882. Much general and useful information on early Northampton personalities.

Historical Catalogue of the Northampton First Church. Northampton, 1891. The vital records of the members of the Northampton Church.

EARLY NORTHAMPTON. Published by Betty Allen Chapter, D.A.R., Northampton, 1914. A collection of papers on early Northampton. Their value and reliability vary considerably.

GREEN, M. A., Springfield 1636-1886. Springfield, 1888. An inadequate history but the best one of this important city.

JUDD, S., History of Hadley. Northampton, 1863. An excellent history of social and economic life in this little Massachusetts town. Unfortunately the absence of an index makes it difficult to use.

PARMENTER, C. O., History of Pelham, 1738-1898. Amherst, Mass. 1898.

PERRY, A. L., Origins in Williamstown, 1900. A scholarly history of the beginning of Williamstown with a good deal of information on western Massachusetts in the middle of the eighteenth century.

SHELDON, GEORGE, History of Deerfield. 2 vols. Deerfield, 1895. A valuable although unreadable history of Deerfield with a good deal on the history of the Connecticut Valley.

TRUMBULL, J. R., History of Northampton Massachusetts. 2 vols. Northampton, 1902. A valuable and useful history of the town. Reprints many original documents, etc.

WELLS, D. W., AND WELLS, R. E., History of Hatfield. Springfield, Mass., 1910.

## SPECIAL STUDIES

AKAGI, R. H., The Town Proprietors of the New England Colonies. Philadelphia, 1921. A valuable and scholarly study of this neglected phase of New England economic organization.

BAILEY, HOLLIS R., Attorneys and their Admission to the Bar in Massachusetts. Boston, 1907. A historical sketch that is particularly useful for the colonial period.

CUSHING, H. A., History of the Transition from the Provincial to Commonwealth Government in Massachusetts. New York, 1896. An excellent study of political movements and developments in Massachusetts between 1774 and 1780.

KINGSLEY, W. L., Yale College. 2 vols. New York, 1879. A poor history of the college although perhaps the best available.

MEYER, J. C., JR., Church and State in Massachusetts, 1740-1833. Cleveland, 1930. A good general account of the movement for religious disestablishment in Massachusetts.

MORRIS, RICHARD B., Studies in the History of American Law with special reference to the Seventeenth and Eighteenth Centuries. New York, 1930. A valuable study of early American legal practices.

PIERCE, BENJAMIN, History of Harvard University. Cambridge, 1833. Gives some interesting information on the founding of "Queen's College."

QUINCY, JOSIAH, The History of Harvard University. 2 vols. Boston, 1860. Brings the story down to 1840. Old-fashioned but still useful.

REYNOLDS, J. B., Two Centuries of Christian Activity at Yale. New York, 1901. Interesting account of the religious life at the institution.

SCHLESINGER, A. M., The Colonial Merchants and the American Revolution 1763-1776, New York, 1917.

SCHUYLER, R. L., Parliament and the British Empire. New York, 1930. A scholarly assertion of parliamentary supremacy over the colonies.

SLY, J. F., Town Government in Massachusetts. Cambridge, 1930. A good discussion and narration of the system of town government.

WASHBURN, EMORY, Sketches of the Judicial History of Massachusetts from 1630 to the Revolution in 1775. Boston, 1840. Mostly a discussion of personalities although the story of development of legal systems in the colony and province is valuable as one of the few that have ever been written.

PUBLICATIONS OF HISTORICAL SOCIETIES

Colonial Society of Massachusetts. 26 vols. 1895-1927. Its *Transactions* and *Collections* are published annually and contain a good deal of general material, both in the form of papers and documents, which is valuable for the colonial history of Massachusetts.

Massachusetts Historical Society. Since 1792, the Society has published its *Proceedings* and *Collections*. The former are composed of papers, miscellaneous documents, and communications presented at the meetings of the Society. The *Collections* are valuable sources of Massachusetts history and have included such things as the Diary of Samuel Sewall, the Warren-Adams Letters, and the Trumbull Papers.

# INDEX

Acadians, The, 82
Adams, John, 45, 46, 48, 124, 126, 134, 135, 136, 155, 174, 175, 180, 190
Adams, Samuel, 102, 105, 111, 114, 117, 124, 126, 135, 136, 145, 154, 158, 160, 162, 171, 174, 175, 180, 189, 190, 192
Allen, Ethan, 149, 150
American Revenue Act of 1764, 100
Amherst, 47
Andros, Governor, 3
Arminianism, 19, 26, 35, 38
Arnold, Benedict, 149, 150, 161, 164, 167
Articles of Confederation, 173
Ashfield, 131, 132
Auchmuty, Robert, 47

Backus, Rev. Isaac, 132
Baptists, The, 130-32
Bardwell, Ebenezer, 60
Belchertown, 55, 57, 60, 62, 107
"Berkshire Affair," 63-68, 107
Berkshire County, 50, 64, 129
Bernard, Francis, 92, 98, 105, 107, 114, 116, 117, 119, 175
Bernardston (Falltown), 62
Bidwell, Adonijah, 16
Billings *vs.* Wood, 55
Blackstone's *Commentaries*, 45, 49
Bliss, George, 44n
"Bloody morning scout, The" (battle of Lake George), 81
Boston, 53, 96, 97, 111, 114, 116, 147, 157, 163
Boston Massacre, 45, 119
Boston Port Bill, 133, 135

Bowdoin, James, 102, 125, 136, 174, 190
"Broken Hints," 138-40
Burgoyne, General John, 173
Cambridge, 19, 20, 24, 98, 117, 119, 120, 145, 149, 151
Canada, 84, 100, 133, 144, 150, 159-60
Canadian expedition, 161-64
Carleton, Sir Guy, 164, 165
Charlestown, N. H. (Number Four), 59, 164, 167
Chauncy, Charles, 20
Clap, Ezra, 11, 14
Clap, Jonathan, 88
Clarke, Joseph, 54, 63, 94, 164, 167
Clark *vs.* Hannum, 58
Claverack, N. Y., 53
Coke, 45, 49, 66
Colrain, 84
Columbia College, 17
*Common Sense*, 156
Confederation, Articles of, 173
Connecticut, 16, 55, 149
Connecticut River, 2, 5, 11, 60
Constitutional Convention, 17, 54
Continental Congress, 17, 135, 136, 140, 147, 151, 152, 154, 157, 158, 160, 169, 170, 173
Conway, 185
Conway, General (Secretary of State), 106
Cooper, Samuel, 127
Crown Point, 79, 80, 165
Curtis, Peter, 64
Cushing, John, 65, 67
Cushing, Thomas, 105, 111, 117, 126, 145, 146, 152, 190

# 210 INDEX

Dana, Richard, 47
Danks, Benoni, 52
De Berdt, Denys, 111
Deerfield, 4, 6
Dieskau, Baron, 80
Dummer, Lieut-Gov. William, 1
Dwight, Timothy, 49
Dyer, Eliphalet, 16

Easthampton, 89
Edwards, Jonathan, 8, 9, 10, 11, 17, 20, 24, 25, 27; opposes Stoddardean System, 28; Hawley's opposition to, 30 ff.; Church council, 3 ff.; Preaches new doctrines, 33; dismissed from Northampton 35; blames Hawley, 36-37; Hawley's apology, 37, 38; at Stockbridge, 39
Ellsworth, Oliver, 17
Ely, Samuel, 185, 187
Eustice, Jane, 52

Falltown (Bernardston), 62
Fonda, Abraham, 53
Forts, Edward, 83; Massachusetts, 70, 75; Pelham, 103; Shirley, 103; William Henry, 83
Franklin, Benjamin, 126, 127, 171
Franklin, John, 64

Gage, General, 135, 136, 141, 143, 145
Gager *vs.* Mattoon, 56
Gates, General, 166, 167
George I, 1
George II, 99
George III, 99, 101, 142
Gerry, Elbridge, 126, 144, 145, 146, 156, 158, 163, 167, 171, 190, 192
Gibbs *vs.* Higgins, 58
Goodman *vs.* Peirce, 58
*Grace Defended*, 20-21
Gray, Harrison, 142, 144
Great Awakening, 9, 26

Great Barrington, 64; Stamp Act riot, 107
Greenleaf, Benjamin, 52
Gridley, Jeremiah, 46
Gunpowder, 163

Hadley, 4, 142, 146, 184
Hall, Rev. Mr., of Sutton, 35, 37
Hampshire County, Court 3, 12, 50; in King George's War, 22; in French and Indian War, 79 ff.; convention in, 142; Whig violence, 146; troops for the Revolution, 164-167; unrest in, 184 ff.; suspension of habeas corpus in, 188; legislative committee investigates, 188; Shays' Rebellion, 190
Hancock, John, 52, 114, 124, 126, 144, 171, 187, 190, 192
Hancock, Thomas, 52
Hartford Convention, 54
Harvard College, 2, 10, 12, 19, 20, 91, 92, 129
Hatfield, 4, 6, 185, 189
Hawley, Elisha, 7, 29, 32, 39, 67, 70, 71, 75, 79, 81
Hawley, Joseph, 2, 3, 4
Hawley, Lieut. Joseph, 2, 4, 5, 9, 10n
Hawley, Major Joseph, ancestry, 2 ff.; childhood, 8 ff.; at Yale, 11 ff.; covenant with God, 18; at Cambridge, 19; his Arminianism, 20, 21, 35, 36, 41; chaplain at Louisbourg, 22, 23; studies law, 23; opposes Jonathan Edwards, 30 ff.; apologizes for part in Edwards affair, 37, 38; admitted to bar, 46; as lawyer, 45-50; law practice, 51 ff.; "Berkshire Affair," 63-68; disbarred, 67, 68; marriage to Mercy Lyman, 74; a major, 76; opposes Israel Wil-

# INDEX 211

liams, 78; in French and Indian War, 79 ff.; a selectman, 87; town clerk, 87; a town proprietor, 88, 89; town schools, 90, 91; marriage, 74; and Queen's College, 91; a deacon, 92; daily life, 92, 93; insanity, 94, 95; work at General Court, 103-5; and compensation for Stamp Act riots, 105-10; and supremacy of Parliament, 108, 111, 124; position at General Court, 119; and boundary settlement, 125; on committee of correspondence, 126; affair of the letters, 126-28; and religious liberty, 129-32, 180; and impeachment of judges, 134, 135; chosen to Continental Congress, 136; advice to John Adams, 136-38; "Broken Hints," 138-40; chairman Northampton Committee of Correspondence, 142; at first Provincial Congress, 143, 144; interest in Canada, 144, 161, 163; mental breakdown, 146, 148; and Ticonderoga, 149, 150; vice-president of Provincial Congress, 151; on Committee of Safety, 151; delegate to Indian Conference, 152; position in Hampshire County, 153, 154; desire for independence, 156-60; need for Continental Government, 159; New England defense, 160; raises troops in Hampshire County, 164-67; on general strategy, 168; and the Tories, 168, 169; final breakdown 170; method of adoption of Constitution, 174-175; and Northampton's criticism of Massachusetts Constitution, 176, 177; his own criticism, 179-82; refuses to act as senator, 182-84; explanation of unrest, 185-87; death, 191; will, 191

Hawley, Mrs. Joseph. *See* Lyman, Mercy

Hawley, Rebekah, 6, 71, 73, 74, 75
Henry, Patrick, 140
Hillsborough, Lord, 114, 122
Hockanum, 8
Hooker, John, 41, 141, 173
Hopkins College, 91
Howe, Lord, 169, 173
Howe, Moses, 60
Hunt, Deacon Ebenezer, 9, 10n
Huntington, Jabez, 17
Hutchinson, Thomas, 44, 49, 65, 66, 67, 101, 102, 107n, 109, 110n, 111, 112, 120, 123, 125, 126, 135, 175, 192

Independence, Declaration of, 160

Jefferson, Thomas, 54, 177
Johnson, Sir William, 80
Johnson, William Samuel, 17
Judd, Jonathan, 189
Judiciary Act of 1789, 17

Kinderhook, N. Y., 83
King George's War, 21
Kingsley, Samuel, 59

Lake George, Battle of, 81
Lanesborough, "Berkshire Affair," 63
Lee, Charles, 144
Leddel, Henry, 53
Leonard *vs.* Cooper, 58
Lincoln, Levi, 54, 174
Livingston, William, 17
Longmeadow, 187
Louisbourg expedition, 21-23
Lyman, Josiah, 62
Lyman, Mercy, 73, 74, 93, 94, 115
Lyman, Phinehas, 16, 23, 47, 48, 80

McLean *vs.* Burbank, 55
Massachusetts, judicial system, 42, 43; town organization, 84-86; government, 96-98, 152; established church in, 130; constitutional convention, 174; constitution of 1780, 175 ff.; breakdown of royal government, 141, 142
Massachusetts Government Act, 141
Massachusetts House of Representatives, circular letter, 113; opposes Quartering Act, 116; adjourned to Cambridge, 117; protests at meeting in Cambridge, 119 ff.; opposes Royal support of Governor, 121; votes impeachment of Justices of Superior Court, 133-35; dissolved by Gage, 136
Massachusetts Provincial Congress, First, 143, Second, 145, and Ticonderoga, 149, 150; committee of safety, 144, 149, 152
Massachusetts-New York boundary, 125, 126
Mather, Cotton, 19
Mather, Increase, 19, 25
Mather, Dr. Samuel, 10, 90
Mayhew, Experience, 20, 21
Merritt, John, 53
Monson, 63
Montgomery, Richard, 161
Morison *vs.* Stewart, 59
Morse (sheriff), 64

New Hampshire, 129, 149, 165, 166
New Haven, 11, 12, 15
New Jersey, 17
New York (Province), 17, 80, 149, 150, 165, 169
Northampton, 1, 4, proprietors in, 85, 86; schools, 90, 91; and compensation for Stamp Act riots, 108; committee of correspondence in, 142; criticism of Mass. Constitution, 176, 177, 179
Number Four (Charlestown, N. H.) 59, 164, 167

Oliver, Andrew, 101, 126
Oliver, Peter, 65, 135, 141
Otis, James, 47, 100, 102, 105, 111, 117

Paine, Robert T., 136
Partridge, Oliver, 59, 78, 79, 91, 142
Pascommuck (Easthampton), 89
Peekskill, 173
Pelham, 60, 61, 75
Pepperell, Lady Mary, 52
Pepperell, Sir William, 52
Percy, Lord, 145; 148
Philadelphia, 138, 144, 151, 155, 162, 169
"Philanthrop," 66
Pittsfield, 64
Pomeroy, Ebenezer, 32; 73
Pomeroy, Elizabeth, 73
Pomeroy, Seth, 22, 23, 53, 79, 81, 143, 170, 173
Porter *vs.* Phelps, 61
Providence, R. I., 53

Quartering Act of 1765, 110, 111, 116 ff.
Quebec, 162
Queens College, 92

Reading, 35
Rhode Island, 69, 70
Root, Martha, 71, 72, 73
Rowe, John, 52
Roxbury, 98

Saltpetre, 163
Scammon, James, 60
Scammon, Samuel, 60
Sedgwick, Theodore, 47, 148, 149

# INDEX 213

Sewall, Samuel, 5, 6
Sewall, Stephen, 129
Shays, Captain Daniel, 190
Shays' Rebellion, 184, 190
Shelburne, Earl of, 113
Shirley, Gov. William, 21, 79, 98
Smith, Abiah, 60
Southampton, 76, 77, 79, 80, 89
South Brimfield, 56
Spooner *vs.* Burt, 55
Springfield, 3, 17, 55, 68, 112, 138, 142, 151, 190
Stamp Act, 63, 101, 102, 105; congress, 17; riot, 107
Stewart, John, 57
Stockbridge, 37, 39
Stoddard, John, 6, 78
Stoddard, Major Solomon, 146, 148, 149
Stoddard, Rev. Solomon, 5, 8, 24, 25
"Stoddardean System," 25, 28
Strong, Caleb, 53, 54, 170, 174, 176, 188
Strong, Simeon, 47
Strong, Thomas, 11
Suffield, 16, 23, 47, 55
Suffolk County, 44, 47
Sugar Act of 1733, 99, 100
Sullivan, James, 47, 48 n, 144, 171, 174, 175, 190
Sutton, 34

Thacher, Oxenbridge, 47, 92
Ticonderoga, 149, 150, 151, 164, 166, 167
Tories, 142, 146, 148, 158, 159, 168, 169, 188
Townshend Acts, 113
*Treatise on Religious Affections* 28

Ware, 61
Warren, James, 126, 169, 171
Warren, Seth, 64, 65, 66
Washington, George, 76, 151, 153, 160, 168, 173
Whitefield, George, 15, 19, 26
Williams, Elisha, 11
Williams, Ephraim, 78, 79, 81
Williams, Israel, 28, 47, 75, 76, 78, 79, 82, 91, 92, 102, 103, 109, 110, 112, 131, 141, 146
Williams, Rev. John, 6
Williams, Rev. Stephen, 23, 187
Williams *vs.* Childs, 58
Williamstown, 75
Winthrop *vs.* Blake, 56
Wood *et al. vs.* Hutchinson, 56
Worcester, 48
Worthington, John, 15, 17, 47, 55, 56, 58, 59, 68, 91, 102, 141, 142
Wright, Ephraim, 185
Wright, Noah, 32

Yale College, 11, 12, 13, 14, 15